Retro

LINDA EVERETT

Beach Bash

A SUN LOVER'S GUIDE TO FOOD AND FUN

PORTLAND, OREGON

Design: Jeff Birndorf, endesign
Editor: Aimee Stoddard

Library of Congress Cataloging-in-Publication Data
Everett, Linda, 1946-
Retro beach bash : a sunlover's guide to food and fun / by Linda Everett.
p. cm.
Includes index.
ISBN 1-888054-75-1
1. Outdoor cookery. 2. Entertaining. I. Title.
TX823 .E94 2003
641.5'78--dc21
2002015239

Printed in Singapore
First American edition
9 8 7 6 5 4 3 2 1

Collectors Press books are available at special discounts for bulk purchases, premiums, and promotions. Special editions, including personalized inserts or covers, and corporate logos, can be printed in quantity for special purposes. For further information contact: Special Sales, Collectors Press, Inc., P.O. Box 230986, Portland OR 97281. Toll free: 1-800-423-1848.

For a free catalog write: Collectors Press, Inc., P.O. Box 230986, Portland, OR 97281. Toll free: 1-800-423-1848 or visit our website at: www.collectorspress.com.

Contents

Introduction

" The beach! The beach! We're going to the beach!" I can remember this chant as we drove our 1956 foam green Pontiac from a Los Angeles suburb to one of our favorite beaches. Huntington, "Tin Can," Laguna, Doheny, Crystal Cove, and Bolsa Chica Beaches all hold wonderful memories for my multi-generational California family.

ack in the 1950s, everyone thought a deep tan was healthy and picnic food always included a little fine sand. We all played in the famous California waves, and although none of us became surfers, we did our share of bodysurfing. I went to two surfer high schools, listening to the Beach Boys in the hallways, surf lingo in the cafeteria, and woodies* in the parking lot.

I still enjoy the beach that is less than a half mile from my home on the world's longest driving beach (28 miles) on the Washington State peninsula. Kites in spectacular sizes and colors fill the sky, sandcastle building is an art and picturesque coves offer prime beachcombing and lighthouse views. When the tourists are gone, the beach belongs once again to us locals. People often sit in saltwater-rusted vehicles at one of the beach overlooks to admire the spectacle of the surf in silence and awe during a storm.

*Woodies are 1950's era station wagons with wood-paneled sides. These became popular as vehicles to haul surfboards to the beach.

Castles in the Sand

Be a Sandcastle Pro

Who says you have to be a kid to enjoy the fun of letting your imagination run amuck in the sand? Ancient Egyptians built sand sculptures over four thousand years ago. Their "castles" were pyramids and obelisks. In the late 1800s, Atlantic City had its own resident sand artists and sandbuilding's popularity took off. Then, the subjects were bas-relief portraits of famous people and events.

irst you need to test the sand's "castle-ability" by tossing a handful around. If it sticks together fairly well, you're ready to begin. The finer the sand is, the better it will stack.

You can pat together a nice crude resemblance of a fort, but if you want to see wonder in the eyes of your kids and smiles from a growing audience, you need the following tools:

1. SHOVEL

An Army surplus folding trenching shovel is great to keep in the trunk of your car.

2. TROWEL

A mason's trowel works well to smooth out walls.

3. BUCKET

A simple 5-gallon plastic one is good for carrying your tools and hauling water. One or two smaller buckets are also handy.

4. KNIFE

No, you aren't going to slice this mudpie! Putty knives, butter knives, and other kinds of knives work well. (Watch the kids!)

8. HOUSEHOLD SPRAY BOTTLE

A spray bottle can be used to finish up, smooth out the sand, and hold the sand together.

9. PLASTIC MOLDS

You could buy some of the commercial molds that eliminate carving, but they soon become limiting and boring. Bring along a nice variety of empty food containers like cottage cheese cartons.

5. MELON BALLER

Perfect for carving out designs, windows, doors and scalloping edges.

6. ICE-CREAM SCOOP

The ice-cream scoop works in much the same way as the melon baller.

7. PAINTBRUSH

Paintbrushes can be used for smoothing surfaces.

SITE

Look for a spot that's on the high edge of the waterline. You want to be able to dig down to the wet sand, but not get flooded out.

BASE

Dig out wet sand from your waterline hole and form a solid flat-topped base.

TOWERS

Swoosh around the sand and some water in the surf or in a bucket. Quickly scoop out a large double handful and let it dribble onto the base, forming a large pancake. The wet mixture gives it stability. Keep adding soppy pancake upon soppy pancake, letting the excess water run down the lower layers. When you get the height you want, start smoothing the tower with the edge of your hand.

WALLS

Instead of soppy pancakes, you now want to make soggy bricks. Mold each handful of wet sand into a brick and lay as you would a real brick wall, staggering each layer over the gap between the layers below. Smooth the wall with your hand, trowel, butter knife, or leave it rugged.

Let your imagination go wild as you carve. Spritz your sculpture with water as necessary to keep it from drying out. You can make your sculpture into anything you want. Your artistic masterpiece can only be limited by the energy and enthusiasm of your construction crew.

If you and your crew are relaxed vacation sand builders, just concentrate on enjoying yourselves. But if the challenge of competition is in your blood, hone your sandcastle skills and try out a contest or two. The first was held July 1952 in Fort Lauderdale, Florida, and competitions can be found on both coasts as well as many lakeside beaches. One of my personal favorites is the "Sandsations" event held here on my own Long Beach, Washington Peninsula, in the month of July.

ONE FINAL NOTE

Please be sure to clean up your beach area, fill in the diggin' hole, and leave the beach pristine for the next creative castler. Sandcastle enthusiasts are also nature lovers and make it a matter of pride to leave the beach cleaner than they found it.

Dragons in the Sky

Kites:
Magic on the End of a String

Over four thousand years ago, a person with imagination and the desire to mimic the graceful flight of birds designed the first kite. After migrating across Asia, the kite, in the form of a 'dragon', became an adult sport in fourteenth-century Europe. Three hundred years later, the diamond kite was brought to the North American continent by sailors traveling the eastern trade routes. These graceful, light, and easy-to-fly kites made kite flying the play of children.

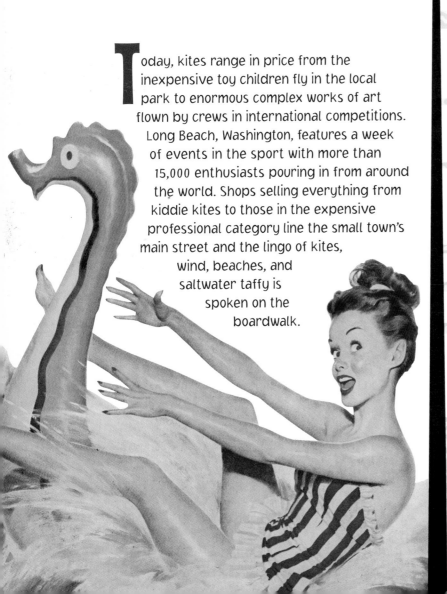

oday, kites range in price from the inexpensive toy children fly in the local park to enormous complex works of art flown by crews in international competitions. Long Beach, Washington, features a week of events in the sport with more than 15,000 enthusiasts pouring in from around the world. Shops selling everything from kiddie kites to those in the expensive professional category line the small town's main street and the lingo of kites, wind, beaches, and saltwater taffy is spoken on the boardwalk.

THERE ARE SEVERAL CATEGORIES OF KITES. HERE ARE A FEW:

1 Box: Pretty much what the name suggests, although there are countless modifications.

2 Delta: A variation of the classic diamond; looks more like a bird.

3 Stunt or Stunter: These come in a variety of shapes, but all have two lines to make them dip and dive and perform controlled acrobatics

4 Sleds: A simple flat six-sided sail.

5 Parafoils: Think of a wing.

6 Windsocks: We know what a windsock is; these imaginative kites come in all sorts of shapes, including creatures like sharks.

There are so many varieties of kites, I recommend first buying a simple one to learn the art of flying. As you become more adept, and hopefully catch the "tako kichi" (kite crazy) bug, you'll want to advance to flying more complex kites. You may also start thinking about making your own. There are several books available with patterns and easy-to-follow directions.

FLYIN'

1 FIRST CHOOSE THE RIGHT SPOT

- Buildings, trees and power lines create obvious problems. The buildings and trees also cause erratic currents and block the wind. Give yourself some space.

- Hills are okay, but fly on the windward side or the turbulence can cause problems.

- Beaches or open fields are the best sites.

2 LAUNCHING

Winds eight to twenty miles per hour make the best kite flying weather. There are three methods of getting your kite off the ground:

(1) Assisted: have a helper hold the kite in front of him or her into the wind while you back off on about 20 feet of line. When you feel a gust of wind your helper turns the kite loose and as it rises, you play out the line.

(2) Single-handed: hold the line and reel in one hand, the kite in the other. When that gust of wind comes along release the kite into the air, tug on the line and as it rises play out the line.

(3) High-start: with your helper holding the kite downwind, keep your line taut and high. If necessary, begin to run as the kite rises into stronger currents.

3 LANDING

Remember to wind the line slowly and steadily. In stronger winds you may have to have your helper hold the reel while you bring the kite in hand-over-hand.

Let's Go Surfin'

There is absolutely nothing like surfing. Well, look at skateboarding or snowboarding and you'll see a resemblance in some of the moves. However, surfing reminds us of those Beach Boy songs, bikini movies, and carefree people having fun. Oh, and don't forget the romance of white beaches and sparkling waves.

The 1950s were the era of enormous change for the surfing world. Until the advent of fiberglass and foam construction in 1958, surfboards had been huge monsters as much as 15 feet long and often made of redwood. Surfboards became lighter, shorter, and quicker. Those cumbersome longboards went the way of the T-Rex, that is, until the 1990s. Many varieties of boards are available now as middle-aged surfers have come back to the beach.

Before taking on the challenge of learning to surf, do your research. Give up all of the ideas you've acquired from old movies (surfers do not say "hey, dude" or "hang ten"). You don't want to start out being labeled a "kook" (beginner). Be aware of the power and unpredictability of the ocean, as well as your limits. The dangers of sharks are nowhere close to the risks of currents, lightning, crashing waves, and your surfboard bopping you on the noggin.

TO START, YOU SHOULD LEARN A LITTLE SURF LINGO

BAGGIES: surf trunks

BLANK: polyurethane core of a surfboard before it gets shaped

BODYBOARD: a short surfboard (about 4 feet long) that you ride lying down in the shorebreak

CONAN: a bodybuilder who hangs around the beach, but doesn't surf

CORD: a short shock-absorbent leash that attaches your ankle to your board

DECK: the upper part of your board where you stand

DING: damage to your board

DROP: taking off on a wave

FACE: the part of the wave you ride

GLASSY: smooth surf without offshore wind

GOOFY FOOT: usually left-handed surfers who ride with their right foot forward

GYRO-SPAZ: a not-so-nice term for someone who really messes up his or her ride on a wave

KOOK: a beginner

LINEUP: the point in the water where you sit and wait to catch a wave

MALLARD: someone who floats around in the lineup like a duck

MUSH: gentle waves that are best for learning

NOSE: the front end of your surfboard

OUTSIDE: looking toward the horizon

OVER THE FALLS: when a surfer gets caught in the break of a wave

PEARL: when the nose of your surfboard dips below the surface and dumps you into the water

RAIL: the side of the surfboard

SET: a series of waves

SLOP: really lousy surf

SOUP: the whitewater (never say whitewater)

SPONGE: a bodyboard

SPONGER/SPONGE RIDER: a person who rides a bodyboard

SURFING IN NEBRASKA: a person who's empty-headed (i.e."That dude's surfing in nebraska.")

SURFWAX: also known as wax; actual wax you rub onto the deck of your surfboard to give you traction

TAIL: the rear of your surfboard

TOES ON THE NOSE: what true surfers say instead of movie surftalk's "hang ten"

TRIM: also known as trimming; when you ride the surfboard at an angle into the wave

TUBE: the tube is formed when a wave breaks and curls over; tubed or tube ride is when you ride inside the tube

Good Clean Fun

While surfing holds the number one spot for excitement, thrills and you-better-believe-it spills, the beach has spawned a fun variety of games, sports and entertainment.

BEACHCOMBING

See special section on this.
(Chapter 5, page 39)

FISHING

Surf fishing is popular for people of all ages. Check with the local bait shop for a tide book. The locals are usually more than helpful with hints on what tackle to use and what's biting on what bait. Fishing piers are terrific fun, especially for the kids. Some are as long as a mile and a half and offer lights for night fishing. California alone has more than ninety piers for fishing fun.

BOOGIE BOARDING

Short surfboard-like boards are ridden while skimming along the edge of the waves.

FRISBEES

Most throwing of this pie pan toy is now between owner and dog instead of sunburned beachnik to beachnik. There are competitions around the country with amazing acrobatics by the four-legged athletes. There are also beaches specifically designated for dogs where they can play off-leash. Remember! Riptides, dangerous surf, and sunburn apply to canines as well as their owners.

HORSEBACK RIDING

This is my personal favorite after beachcombing. Stables in certain areas offer safe, guided trips of all lengths, even half-day and all-day with picnic lunches. If you choose to go with your own horse, check into boarding facilities and campgrounds that will accept them. As with your kids and canine pals, respect the safety and etiquette rules of the sand and surf.

IN-LINE SKATING

Although you aren't going to skate across that white sand, many beachside areas are crammed with skaters whizzing down the boardwalks and sidewalks. I've had to dodge many.

KITE FLYING

See special section on this. (Chapter 2, page 17)

SKATE-BOARDING

Maybe you don't think of this as a beach sport, but look at the style and even the name.

VOLLEYBALL

Santa Monica Beach, California, was the legendary beginning of beach volleyball in the 1920s. During World War II, our soldiers played the game on faraway tropical beaches and brought it to popularity.

Volleyball became an official sport when it was played at the Olympics, starting in 1964. Like surfing, this sport has its own lingo; dinks, hammers, slams, spikes, facial spikes, and lollipops are just a few you'll hear. Basically, these words describe various ways of smashing the ball at or (as in the self-explanatory facial spike!) into your opponent.

WHALE WATCHING

Starting around Christmas time, these glorious monoliths of the sea migrate south from the cold of Alaska to Mexico's Baja to bear their young. Humpbacks, Grays, flashy Orcas (Killer Whales), and the planet's largest animal, the Great Blue, put on a show all along the west coast. Take a tour boat or hang out at one of the coast's designated watching points (some with guides); have your binoculars in hand for the thrill of a lifetime.

WINDSURFING

In the 1960s, an avid surfer and his sailing pal patented the fusion of their favorite sports. The sail works on a universal joint, which the windsurfer tilts to steer and catch the wind. In 1984, windsurfing hit the big time in the Olympics and a World Tour.

A few more sports to consider are sailing, boating, parasailing, kayaking, scuba diving, snorkeling, and bird watching. Your local library should provide all the information you need.

Footprints in the Sand
Beachcombing

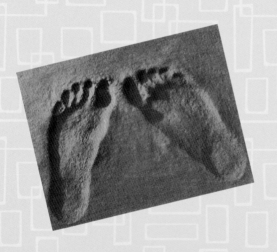

Beachcombing is a treasure hunt. Strolling down a sandy stretch, perhaps the morning after a big storm, you will find all sorts of riches and rewards from pieces of driftwood that can easily pass for artwork to keepsake bottles that have traveled many currents. Beachcombing has numerous pleasures, not the least of which is the meditation-like serenity you will experience while walking by the sea. And it's all free.

HERE ARE SOME TREASURES TO LOOK FOR:

AGATES AND OTHER STONES

Certain beaches all up and down the west coast are prime spots for many types of semiprecious stones such as agates, jasper, and even jade. The best hunting is in gravel beds that have been uncovered by winter storms.

BOTTLES

We would all like to find a note in a bottle that has drifted upon exotic currents for untold years. Occasionally one may be found. Or perhaps you will find a Greek, Portuguese, Spanish, French, Russian, or Asian wine bottle with decorative embossing and unusual labels.

DRIFTWOOD

There is no limit to the beauty nature can produce using a piece of wood, water, waves, and sand. This is Mother Nature's sculpture and you get to choose.

FLOATS

Many beachcombers agree that those wonderful old hand-blown glass floats from Japan are number one on their list of treasures. The size ranges up to a huge two to three feet in diameter; most are between four inches and a foot. The colors vary, but green, clear, and blue are most common. A few floats were made in the United States around World War II and used as crab pot markers. The rumor that glass is being replaced by plastic is untrue; several glass factories in Japan and Korea are still active. European countries still use floats, though on a smaller scale.

OTHER FLOATS

Although not as beautiful and desirable as the glass ones, plastic, foam, wood, and cork floats come in a fun variety of shapes and colors. On the Long Beach Washington Peninsula, these crab pot and fishing floats hang from many fences and even trees.

SALVAGE

A few hardy 'combers make a tidy extra income by hitting the beaches before the crowd strictly to locate salvageable items. This may include lumber, logs, or other cargo that has broken free in rough seas and washed ashore. Just such a load of logs recently became a bonanza for a salvager on a beach only a few blocks from me. Be careful that you aren't hauling off materials that have been sold by an insurance company to a professional salvage company.

SHIP DEBRIS
(SEE ALSO SALVAGE)

This debris could include life preservers, tackle blocks, mooring lines, hatches, and just about anything that a ship may discard or that has washed ashore from a wreck.

MISCELLANEOUS

Miscellaneous items could range from ancient walrus ivory on a remote beach in Alaska to a shipment of name-brand tennis shoes that washed ashore here a few years ago (there was a central clearing area for these so people could locate the matching shoes).

WHILE OUT LOOKING FOR TREASURES, HERE ARE SOME BEACHCOMBING HINTS

1

4
Choose flat beaches with heavy surf rather than steep beaches.

2
Beachcomb during and after storms, especially after sustained onshore winds (winter and spring storms are most productive).

3
Beachcombing is best on Thursdays after the Monday through Wednesday high tide accumulation of debris.

The Word is Safer, Not Surfer

Remember!
Nature is not a theme park!

SUN · SURF · WILDLIFE · DRIVING

THE SUN

By now, we all know that sunburn is most definitely not good for our skin. Yes, that great tan looks wonderful and an occasional mild sunburn may seem harmless, but medical research describes the dangers of exposure to the sun. That hazy beachside day may lure you into thinking the sun has no fire, but that's not true. In the northern hemisphere, the harmful UV, or ultraviolet, radiation is highest in the summer between 10 a.m. and 2 p.m. Water and sand reflect even more sunlight, thus increasing your exposure. Take extra measures when beachcombing, fishing, or just enjoying the view.

HERE ARE A FEW TIPS TO KEEP YOUR SKIN BEAUTIFUL AND CANCER-FREE

1 Use a good waterproof suntan lotion with SPF (sun protection factor) of at least 15. Look for a brand that has protects against both UVA and UVB rays. Apply more lotion as often as needed.

2 Use suntan lotion on babies (over six months) and young children with a higher SPF (30) and made specifically for their delicate skin. However, it's a better idea to simply keep them shielded from the sun.

3 Wear a hat with a wide brim. This is especially crucial for small children.

4 Limit your amount of sun exposure for tanning to fifteen minutes per day.

5 Cover up! Wear a light cotton shirt with sleeves.

6 Use a beach umbrella stuck in the sand or one of those clever umbrellas that attach to your folding chair.

7 Wear Sunglasses!

8 Be sure to wear protective clothing and sunscreen all year round.

THE SURF

If you're basking and dunking on a beach that has lifeguards, check out the colored flags flying from their stations:

Green—safe to swim
Yellow—use caution; there could be rough surf
Red—no swimming
Blue—stinging jellyfish are present

Here are a few other items for which you should be on the lookout. Sometimes lifeguards will display flags warning of these dangers as well.

LOGS

The power of the surf can take an enormous log and roll it right over you. Don't let your kids play on logs, especially those near the surf's edge. Drifted logs are also dangerous; they can be located on teetering perches by storm-powered surf. Driftwood can also be slippery and slimy and cause you to lose your footing.

RIPTIDES

These treacherous tides form a strong current which surges through sandbars on the ocean floor. No matter how strong of a swimmer you are, you can't swim against a riptide. Drift with the current and let the wave action bring you in. Don't hesitate to get help.

SANDBARS AND STREAM BANKS

Many beaches have enticing sandbars where 'combing looks good. However, the footing on both sandbars and storm-eroded banks may be treacherous.

SNEAKER WAVES

Sneaker waves are the most dangerous and unpredictable surf, usually found on flat sandy beaches and on other beaches at low tide. There is no warning of these rough, powerful waves that smash ashore, picking up everything in their way. The water level can be raised as much as ten feet. Sneaker waves kill as they sweep beachcombers or waders off their feet or crush them with a previously picturesque log.

52

STORMS

Although beachcombing during a storm is recommended for finding treasures, be aware of your limits. Only consider going if you and your partner (never go alone) are knowledgeable about waves, tides, and weather. Dress appropriately!

TIDES

Be aware of the tides! Don't clamber out on a group of rocks or along a steep cliff and find yourself stranded by incoming waters.

Here are some fun weather facts that can also help to plan your beachside time as well as safety.

1 A red morning sun forecasts rain to come soon.

2 A red evening sun forecasts a nice day tomorrow.

3 A greenish or yellowish sky forecasts rain.

4 A late afternoon rainbow forecasts clear weather for tomorrow.

5 A small ring around the sun or moon forecasts rain within a few hours.

6 Twinkling stars forecast rain.

7 A pale moon forecasts rain.

8 A red moon forecasts increasing winds.

9 A bright white moon forecasts fair weather.

10 Long waves and increasing swells forecast a storm from the direction of the waves.

WILDLIFE

EEEK! IT'S A . . .

It's important to remember that we share that sparkling sand—especially in the more remote areas where beachcombing is best—with a variety of wildlife. Most are harmless; a few are not. So, enjoy watching the animals from a distance.

Please note that baby seals rest on the beach and are not abandoned. If you hang around them, momma will not return.

DRIVING

Beach driving is indescribable. There's something very freeing about driving down a wide expanse, no lines, no shoulder, waves sneaking at you on one side, flocks of birds skittering off into a postcard sunset.

HERE ARE JUST A FEW HINTS AND THINGS TO REMEMBER

1 Only a few beaches allow driving.

2 Read all signs carefully for:
- A. speed limit
- B. closing times, days or months (our beach is closed for the breeding season of the rare Plover bird)
- C. warnings of dangerous areas
- D. specific closed areas (wildlife preserves, private property, etc.)

3 Always keep one eye on the surf. (See pages 50-52).

4 Keep to the hard wet sand and avoid the soft dry sand, especially at the edge of dunes and beach approaches.

5 Do not drive in the dunes or wetlands.

6 Do not litter!

7 Use extra caution when passing other vehicles.

8 Be aware that there are usually a lot of beachgoers and dogs to look out for.

9 Use caution when crossing any creeks or driving in the surf. There may be crabholes, crumbling banks and drop-offs.

10 Remember to hose off your vehicle soon after you leave the beach. The saltwater will corrode the paint.

Picnic Provisions

Southern (California) Fried Chicken

2 broiler/fryer chickens (about 3 pounds each),
    cut into serving pieces
2 cups all-purpose flour
1/4 tsp salt
1 tsp pepper
4 cups vegetable oil
approximately 2 tsps. salt

marinade

2 cups vegetable oil
2 eggs, beaten
1 tsp dried oregano
1 tsp dried rosemary
1 tsp dried tarragon
1 tsp paprika
2 cloves garlic, crushed

Serves 8-10

Rinse the chicken and pat dry with paper towels. Place in a shallow baking dish. In a small bowl, combine the ingredients for the marinade: vegetable oil, eggs, oregano, rosemary, tarragon, paprika and garlic. Mix well. Pour marinade over chicken, turning pieces to coat thoroughly. Let marinate about 2 hours in refrigerator, covered. Mix flour with salt and pepper. You'll need 2 large heavy skillets. Pour 2 cups vegetable oil in each skillet and heat until a drop of water sizzles in the oil. Brown the chicken quickly in oil on all sides. Salt to taste as you fry chicken. When all pieces are golden brown, cover skillets, turn down heat and continue cooking until chicken is tender, about another 20 minutes.

Sunburned Skewered Beef

4 pound boneless chuck roast
meat tenderizer (non-salt variety)
Honolulu marinade (recipe follows)
$1/4$ cup butter or margarine, melted
5 medium-sized ears of corn, husked and cut into 2-inch lengths
3 medium green peppers, seeded and cut into $1 1/2$-inch chunks
2 large sweet onions, red are okay, cut into $1 1/2$-inch chunks
1 medium pineapple (about 3 pounds), peeled, cored, and cut into $1 1/2$-inch cubes

Cut chuck roast across grain into cubes about $1 1/2$ inches square. Sprinkle generously with tenderizer. Place in a shallow baking dish and cover with marinade. Turn pieces to coat. Cover and refrigerate for at least 6 hours or overnight. In a small bowl, combine butter or margarine, and $1/3$ cup marinade. Discard remaining marinade. Thread meat on skewers alternating with corn, green pepper, onion, and pineapple. Brush butter mixture over chunks on skewer. Grill over hot coals basting frequently with butter mixture.

Serves 8-12

Honolulu Marinade

$1 1/2$ cups pineapple juice
$1 1/2$ cups dry red wine
$1 1/2$ tblsps dried instant onion
$1 1/2$ tsp dried thyme
$3/4$ tsp dry mustard
$1/4$ cup brown sugar, firmly packed
$1/4$ tsp pepper
2 cloves, garlic, crushed

In a medium bowl mix pineapple juice, wine, onion, thyme, mustard, brown sugar, pepper, and garlic together.

Serves 4-6

Sandbar Clam Chowder for a Crowd

This recipe is geared for a crowd like you might have at a Fourth of July bash. Consider going together with friends and enjoying the fireworks, sitting on driftwood around the bonfire, and feasting on this beach classic.

3 gallons cream or half and half
2 pounds butter (I didn't say this was low cal)
1 cup all-purpose flour
10 onions, finely chopped
$2 1/2$ bunches celery, finely chopped
1/2 cup salt
1 tblsp pepper
1/4 cup celery seed
10 pounds potatoes (I prefer white), cooked, peeled, diced
2 cans (8 oz.) clam juice
3 pounds clams, finely chopped

In a large saucepan, bring cream or half and half to a gentle boil. In a smaller pan, melt $1 1/2$ pounds of butter and stir in flour to make a roux. Stir flour mixture into cream to make a cream sauce. In a big deep pot, heat remaining $1/2$ pound butter and sauté onion and celery until tender. Add in salt, pepper, and celery seed. Add potatoes, clam juice, clams, and cream sauce to vegetables and heat thoroughly, about 10 minutes. Stir often to be sure it doesn't scorch.

Serves 30

One-Pan Pasta
(a.k.a. "Camper's Super Goop")

This simple take-along dish can be "dressed up, dressed down, or dressed all around," as my kids say. Begin with the basic dish and venture into the assorted options as the mood takes you. It's delicious prepared over a campfire or in your RV.

1 tblsp vegetable or olive oil
1 medium onion, finely chopped (or 1 tblsp, dried onion)
1 garlic clove (medium to large according to your taste)
1 pound lean ground beef
1 can (28 oz.) diced tomatoes with juice
1 cup red wine
$\frac{1}{2}$ cup water
1 tsp oregano
$\frac{1}{2}$ tsp garlic powder
1 tsp salt
4 oz. thin spaghetti
grated Parmesan cheese

Serves 4–6

In a medium skillet, heat the oil and sauté onion and garlic clove until tender but not browned. Add in the ground meat and continue cooking until browned, breaking up with a fork. Add in the can of tomatoes, red wine, water, oregano, garlic powder, and salt. Bring to a boil and cook one minute. Reduce heat to low and simmer covered for 25 minutes more. Stir occasionally. Cook spagehetti according to package directions, drain well. Top with the sauce and parmesan cheese to taste.

options:
$\frac{1}{2}$ cup chopped pepperoni
$\frac{1}{2}$ cup chopped Italian salami
$\frac{1}{2}$ cup cooked Italian hot or sweet sausage (polska kielbasa or bratwurst works)
$\frac{1}{2}$ cup sautéed green, red, or yellow peppers
1 tblsp Italian seasoning (adjust oregano, garlic powder, and salt in basic recipe)
$\frac{1}{2}$ to 1 cup grated cheddar or other favorite cheese
$\frac{1}{2}$ cup sautéed mushrooms or one small (4 oz.) can

Sun Baked Casserole

Serve this casserole with a crispy salad. A loaf of crusty garlic bread, sourdough, sourdough rye or other favored variety grilled on the side of the coals makes a complete meal.

1 pound lean ground beef
6 cups water
1 medium onion, chopped (or 1 tblsp dried)
1 tsp garlic salt
1 package (8 oz.) wide egg noodles
1 tblsp Worcestershire sauce
1 tblsp fresh chives, finely chopped (1 1/2 tsp dried)
1/2 cup cottage cheese
1/2 pint sour cream

In a deep pot, sauté the ground beef over medium high heat until browned. Break it up as it cooks. Add in the water and bring to a boil. Add in the onion, garlic salt and noodles. Turn heat down to medium and cook uncovered until noodles are tender. Spoon off any excess water. Reduce heat to low. Stir in the Worcestershire sauce, chives, cottage cheese and sour cream, stirring until just hot.

Serves 4–6

Time-Proven Batter for Your Catch

In order to make true fish and chips, you'll need to use lard. British "chips" are actually potatoes cut into chunks and fried in lard. And, yes, the only way to get that flavor is to use the hot lard.

1 cup all-purpose flour
1 egg yolk
5 tblsps beer
1/4 tsp salt
6 tblsps milk
6 tblsps water
2 egg whites

Serves 4–6

Pour flour into a medium bowl. Make a well in the center and add in egg yolk, beer and salt. Mix well. Mix milk and water together and add to flour mixture gradually, stirring until smooth. Beat egg whites until firm peaks form. Fold into flour mixture. Dip fish pieces into batter and fry in hot oil.

BEACH BUNDLES

These packet meals are perfect for beachside campfires. I remember learning how to make them in the Girl Scouts. They're quick, easy and the possibilities are limitless. You can even serve the meal in its own foil dish.

Hush Them Dawgs

If you don't mind the extra work, these traditional corn meal dabs go perfectly with that batter fried fish.

2 ¹/₂ cups corn meal
1 tsp onion powder or 2 tsp onion, finely chopped
1 tsp salt
1 tsp baking soda
1 ¹/₂ cups buttermilk
2 cups vegetable oil

In a large bowl combine corn meal, onion, salt, and baking soda. Add in buttermilk and mix until stiff (corn meal will swell). In your Dutch oven or deep cast iron skillet, heat oil until a teaspoon of the batter bubbles and sizzles when dropped in the oil. Drop heaping tablespoons of batter into oil. Don't crowd. Cook until golden brown. Remove and drain on paper towels. Serve with butter or dip in baked bean juices or dip in soup. These will disappear as fast as you can cook 'em.

Serves 4–6

Corona del Mar Clambake

Seaweed (optional, but gives flavor and ambiance)
24 steamer clams, scrubbed clean
1 ¹/₂ pounds crab legs
1 small broiler/fryer chicken (about 2 pounds), cut in pieces
2 large ears of corn, husked and quartered
2 small sweet onions, quartered
2 medium potatoes, cut lengthwise in quarters
¹/₂ tsp salt
¹/₄ tsp pepper
¹/₂ cup melted butter

Serves 8

Tear off eight large pieces of heavy-duty aluminum foil. If you're using seaweed, place a small handful on each sheet of foil. If you don't use seaweed, add ¹/₄ cup water to packet before sealing cosed. Divide up the clams, crab, and chicken between packets. Stuff in corn, onion, and potato where there's space. Season with salt and pepper then drizzle with butter. Seal up each packet and grill over medium-hot coals for 45 minutes to 1 hour or until chicken is tender. Open a packet (careful, it's steamy and hot) and test chicken for doneness. Serve with individual bowls of garlic butter for dipping.

Channel Islands Chicken Pack

1 broiler/fryer chicken (3 to 3 ½ pounds), quartered
¼ cup butter or margarine
1 envelope (1 ½ oz.) onion soup mix
1 tsp paprika
1 can (4 oz.) mushroom stems and pieces, drained

Rinse chicken, pat dry, and remove skin and fat. Tear off 4 sheets of heavy-duty aluminum foil. On each piece of foil, place one quarter of the chicken and sprinkle with 1 tsp butter, 1 tblsp soup mix, and ¼ tsp paprika. Divide mushrooms in fourths and add on top of chicken. Bring up foil and fold into a sealed packet over chicken. Grill over medium-hot coals for about 45 minutes, turning packet every 10 minutes

 Serves 4

Peggy's Portside Pot Roast

1 package (½ oz.) Italian salad dressing mix
¼ cup all-purpose flour
1 tsp salt
½ tsp paprika
¼ tsp pepper
1 beef blade pot roast (about 3 to 4 pounds) 2 cups carrots, thinly sliced
2 cups zucchini, thinly sliced
2 cups potatoes, thinly sliced

Serves 8-10

In a small bowl, combine salad dressing mix, flour, salt, paprika, and pepper. Mix well. Place roast in the center of a double sheet of heavy-duty aluminum foil. Coat both sides of the meat with dressing mix. Bring foil up around meat and seal well. Grill over medium hot coals for 1 ½ hours, turning after 1 hour. Remove packet from coals, open carefully and place carrots, zucchini, and potatoes on roast. Reseal packet and return to grill over medium hot coals. Do not turn packet. Cook about 30 minutes.

Seafarer's Fast Fish

(per person)
1 slice lean bacon
½ pound of a nice firm boneless fish, fillet or chunks
1 medium-sized white or red potato, quartered
½ sweet onion, sliced thick
½ tsp salt
¼ tsp pepper
½ clove garlic, finely chopped

On a sheet of heavy-duty aluminum foil, place ½ slice bacon with fish on top. Top with remaining bacon and cover with potato and onion. Sprinkle salt, pepper, and garlic over all. Seal foil. Grill over indirect heat for 15 to 20 minutes on each side. Serve with green salad and sourdough bread grilled over the coals.

SANDWICHES/BREADS

What could be simpler to make, please any crowd, fit any budget, and be easier to transport than the invention the fourth Earl of Sandwich blessed us with? Personally, I believe his stable hands had slapped meat between hunks of bread ages before and the Earl just got the credit. Here are a few sandwich suggestions with a few that may slide into the category of fancier fare.

San Francisco Oyster Loaf

1 large loaf (16 oz.) sourdough bread
1 cup butter, melted
2 dozen medium oysters
1 cup fine dry bread crumbs, unseasoned
3 eggs, slightly beaten
$^1/_2$ tsp salt
$^1/_4$ tsp pepper
1 small lemon, thinly sliced
$^1/_4$ cup fresh parsley, chopped

Serves 4–6

Slice off top of bread lengthwise, save. Hollow out loaf then brush generously on inside with butter, but reserve some of the butter for later (about $^1/_2$ cup). Bake bread in a 400 degree oven until hot and lightly toasted. While bread is heating, roll oysters first in breadcrumbs, then in beaten egg and again in crumbs. In a heavy skillet, fry oysters in reserved butter. Fry on both sides, but don't overcook; 4 to 5 minutes is fine. Season oysters with salt and pepper. Fill the hot crusty loaf with the fried oysters and drizzle a little of the leftover butter/juice from frying pan over them. Cover with the lemon slices and sprinkle parsley over all. Place toasted lid on loaf and serve. Spoon out oysters first, then slice the bread and pass around.

Sandbar Sandwich

1 cup cheddar cheese, grated (you
    could use Monterey Jack or
    another favorite)
$1/2$ tsp sweet onion, grated
$1/2$ tsp Worcestershire sauce
1 can (12 oz.) condensed tomato soup
1 can (6 oz.) shrimp (broken is fine),
    imitation lobster, or crabmeat,
    drained and flaked
$1/4$ cup mayonnaise (adjust according
to how moist you like it)
6 English muffins

In a medium bowl, combine cheese,
onion, Worcestershire sauce, soup,
shrimp or crab, and mayonnaise. Toast
muffins lightly on grill and top with
filling. Wrap in foil and bake on outer
edge of coals for about 15 minutes.

Serves 4-6

Waterfront Willie's Sausage Rolls

8 large pork sausages (if you have spicier tastes, try Italian hot or
    sweet varieties)
6 tblsps olive oil
6 green bell peppers, thinly sliced (I like to mix in
    some red and yellow for sweetness and color)
3 sweet onions, thinly sliced (Walla Wallas, Maui, or Vidalia if you can)
Kaiser or sourdough rolls

Serves 8

Poke each of the sausages with a fork to release the fat. Brown them in a skillet
until thoroughly cooked. Pour off fat. Drain on paper towels. Add in the olive oil
and sauté peppers and onions until tender but not browned. Add in the cooked
sausages and simmer 15 to 20 minutes, spooning off any excess fat. Spoon into
rolls and hand out to eager picnickers.

Say Pizza Please

Everyone knows how kids love pizza
and a lot of us grown-ups, too. Think
of pizza in the form of a sandwich
and there are unlimited possibilities.

8 slices thick sourdough or French
    bread
$1/4$ cup olive oil
2 medium cloves of garlic

$1/2$ tsp each oregano and garlic salt
    (or Italian seasoning mix)
8 slices Italian salami or equal
    amount of pepperoni
8 oz. Mozzarella cheese, thinly
    sliced into 8 slices
8 thick slices of tomato

Toast bread to light golden brown.
Brush one side of each slice with olive
oil. Peel garlic clove and slice off stem

end. Lightly scrub garlic clove over
oiled side of toasted bread. Follow
with a light sprinkling of either a pre-
mixed Italian seasoning blend or the
oregano and garlic salt. On oiled side
of toasted bread, place one slice of
salami, a slice of cheese topped by a
slice of tomato. If you make these in
your RV, you can end with the cheese
and broil for a couple of minutes until
the cheese is slightly melted.

Serves 4-6

Buccaneer Buns

These "bunwiches" can be made ahead at home, kept cold in your RV refrigerator or chest cooler, and heated in foil on the edge of your grill or campfire.

1 can (6 oz.) flaked tuna, or ½ cup leftover chicken or turkey
¼ pound American cheese, grated
3 hard-boiled eggs, grated
½ cup mayonnaise
2 tblsps green pepper, chopped
2 tblsps sweet onion, chopped
2 tblsps stuffed green olives, chopped
2 tblsps pickle relish
6 hamburger or similar buns

In a medium bowl, combine tuna, cheese, eggs, mayonnaise, green pepper, onion, olives, and relish. Fill buns, wrap in foil, and chill. Heat on edge of grill or campfire for about 5 minutes.

Serves 6

Tidewater Billy's Toast

8 oz. (2 cups) jack cheese, grated
8 oz. (2 cups) cheddar cheese, grated
1 small can (4 oz.) chopped green chilies
½ cup mayonnaise
½ tsp salt
1 clove garlic, finely chopped, or 1 tsp minced from a jar (adjust to your taste)
1 large (1 pound) loaf French or sourdough bread, unsliced

In a large bowl combine cheeses, chilies, mayonnaise, salt, and garlic. Split bread in half lengthwise and grill until lightly toasted. Place each half on a sheet of heavy foil and spread with the cheese mixture. Fold over foil and heat on edge of grill or campfire. Goes great with a green salad.

Serves 4–6

Copper River Salmon Sandwich

8 slices rye bread, thinly sliced
1 package (8 oz.) cream cheese, slightly softened
8 thin slices smoked salmon
1 small sweet onion, very thinly sliced

Serves 4

Spread all slices of the bread with cream cheese. Top with a slice of salmon followed by a slice of onion. Put together and cut in half.

Variation:
In place of cream cheese, use softened butter. Add on a very thin slice of ripe tomato. Sprinkle the salmon with lemon juice.

71

Mexicali Chicken San'

1 ripe avocado, mashed
1 tsp lime or lemon juice
1 tblsp onion, finely chopped
2 tblsps mayonnaise
8 Hoagie, Kaiser or similar rolls
    (good hot dog buns will work)
1 cup cooked chicken, chopped
$^{1}/_{2}$ cup lettuce, shredded

In a small bowl, mix together the avocado,
juice, onion, and mayonnaise. Fill each bun
with the mixture, top with chicken followed
by lettuce.

Serves 8

Baja Bay Sandwich

3 oz. cream cheese, softened
dash of chili powder
$^{1}/_{2}$ tsp fresh cilantro, chopped
$^{1}/_{4}$ cup black olives, chopped
    (add more if you like; you can also
    try stuffed green olives)
8 slices raisin bread
4 slices cooked chicken,
    (8 if they're thin)

In a small bowl, mix together the cream
cheese, chili powder, and cilantro. Blend
in the olives. Spread this mixture on 4
of the bread slices and top with a slice
or 2 of chicken followed by the other 4
slices of bread.

Serves 4

SIDEKICKS (SALADS AND SIDE DISHES)

Seafarer's Slaw

1 medium head cabbage, shredded (to make the slaw more colorful substitute 1/3 with red cabbage)
1 tblsp sugar
3 tblsps apple cider vinegar
2 tblsps sweet onion, finely chopped
1 carrot, shredded
1/4 cup red or green pepper, finely chopped
3 stalks celery, thinly sliced
1 small can (8 oz.) pineapple tidbits, drained (save juice)
1/4 cup mayonnaise

In a large bowl, shred cabbage. Sprinkle with sugar and vinegar and toss. Let stand for 10 or 15 minutes. Drain cabbage well. In a medium bowl, combine onion, carrot, red or green pepper, celery, and pineapple. Mix with cabbage. Combine enough pineapple juice with mayonnaise to make a dressing about the consistency of canned milk. Toss with cabbage mixture.

Serves 10

Man Overboard Potato Salad

5 pounds potatoes (I prefer white or red), cooked, peeled (if russet type), cubed and chilled
6 hard-boiled eggs, peeled and chopped
3 medium sweet pickles or 1/4 cup sweet relish
1/2 cup black olives, sliced
1/2 cup green onion or sweet onion, thinly sliced
1/2 cup celery, thinly sliced
1 cup mayonnaise
1/2 cup sour cream
3 tsp prepared mustard
1 tsp garlic salt
1/4 tsp pepper
1/2 tsp paprika

Serves 10-12

In a large bowl, toss together potatoes, eggs, pickles, olives, onion, and celery. In a small bowl, blend together mayonnaise, sour cream, mustard, salt, and pepper. Mix dressing with potato mixture. If needed, add more mayonnaise. Garnish top of salad with paprika. Keep salad well chilled.

Snappy German Potato Salad

1 can (15 oz.) sliced new potatoes, drained and rinsed
3 tblsps vinegar
3 tblsps olive oil
1/2 tsp garlic salt
1/4 tsp pepper
3 tblsps fresh chives, finely chopped
1/2 large cucumber (approximately 1/2 cup), peeled and chopped
1 small sweet onion, finely chopped
1/2 cup mayonnaise (adjust according to your taste)

In a medium bowl, toss together potatoes, vinegar, oil, garlic salt, pepper, chives, cucumber, and onion; mix in mayonnaise. Chill overnight if possible to blend flavors.

Serves 4-6

73

Red's Famous Bean Salad

2 cans (15 oz.) red kidney beans, drained and rinsed
1 cup cucumbers, peeled and chopped
1 cup celery, chopped
$^1/_2$ cup green pepper, chopped
$^1/_2$ cup sweet onion, chopped
Your favorite mild Italian dressing

In a medium bowl, combine the kidney beans, cucumbers, celery, green pepper, and onion. Pour approximately $^1/_2$ cup dressing over salad and toss well. Chill before serving.

Serves 12

Plain Darn Simple Salad

2 tblsps olive oil
3 tblsps apple cider vinegar
$^1/_2$ tsp garlic powder
$^1/_2$ tsp salt
$^1/_4$ tsp pepper
3 large ripe tomatoes (Beefsteak are great)
1 medium red onion, sliced as thin as possible

In a medium bowl, toss together the olive oil, vinegar, garlic, salt, pepper, tomatoes, and onion. Chill overnight if possible.

Serves 6-8

Greek Creek Campground Salad

$^1/_4$ cup extra virgin olive oil
3 tblsps lemon juice
1 garlic clove, minced
1 tsp salt
1 tsp pepper
1 tsp tarragon
1 tsp dried parsley (or 1 tblsp fresh)
3 cups assorted chopped vegetables: mushrooms, green pepper, red pepper, yellow pepper, artichoke hearts, raw green beans, zucchini, celery, or cauliflower

In a large pan, heat together the olive oil, lemon juice, garlic, salt, pepper, tarragon, and parsley. Add in the vegetables and stir to coat with mixture. Add in just enough water to cover and simmer on low heat for about 15 minutes or until vegetables are still crisp. Chill in the liquid, preferably overnight. Drain and serve.

Serves 6-8

Campfire Biscuits

2 cups prepared biscuit mix
   (such as Bisquick)
$^1/_4$ cup powdered milk
$^2/_3$ cup water

Before going on your camping trip, mix several batches of this. Mix together the biscuit mix and powdered milk in a large zip-top plastic storage bag. At sunrise, add enough water (approximately $^2/_3$ cup) to make a stiff dough. Meanwhile get those lazy campers up. Hand each one a tree limb (making sure it isn't something poisonous like Yew or Hemlock) you've prepared at home by removing the bark. The limb should be about $^3/_4$ inch in diameter and 2 feet long. Form the dough around end of the limb, making "biscuits" about 3 inches long and 2 inches wide. Toast biscuits over the campfire until golden brown. Slip off of limb and fill cavity with butter and honey or jam.

Serves 4–6

Landlubber Beans

$^1/_2$ pound lean bacon or ham
1 large onion, chopped
1 can (15 oz.) butter beans, undrained
1 can (15 oz.) can pork and beans
1 can (15 oz.) can kidney beans,
   drained
1 can (15 oz.) can baked beans
$^1/_2$ cup firmly packed brown sugar
2 tsp Worcestershire sauce
$^1/_2$ cup catsup

Cook bacon until crisp, drain, and cut into bite-sized pieces. In leftover bacon fat, cook onion until tender. Drain off fat. In a large casserole dish, combine beans, bacon, onions, sugar, Worcestershire sauce, and catsup. Bake at 325 degrees for 1 $^1/_2$ hours, or bake on the side of your campfire in a cast-iron kettle or in your Dutch oven nestled in the coals with a few more embers on top. The latter makes the best-flavored beans.

Serves 12–16

Drunken Sailor Beans

These beans are a wonderful accompaniment to just about any picnic or barbecue meat, but especially ribs, burgers, and dogs.

2 cans (28 oz. each) baked beans
1 $^1/_2$ tsp dry mustard
3 tblsps dark molasses (use the light molasses if you like a less intense flavor)
$^1/_2$ cup chili sauce
$^1/_2$ cup strong coffee
$^1/_2$ cup bourbon
1 can (8 oz.) sliced pineapple
$^1/_4$ cup dark brown sugar (use the light brown version if you like)

In a medium bowl, mix together beans, mustard, molasses, chili sauce, coffee, and bourbon. Put in a buttered baking dish and let stand overnight so flavors can blend. Bake uncovered, for 40 minutes at 375 degrees. Top with a layer of pineapple sprinkled with the brown sugar. Bake for an additional 40 minutes uncovered. These beans are terrific with crusty sourdough, Boston Brown Bread, or rolls for soppin' up the delectable sauce.

Serves 10

Bayou Beach Black-eyed Peas

2 quarts boiling water
1 pound dried black-eyed peas
1 medium onion, chopped
1/2 pound lean bacon, cut into 1/2-
    inch cubes
1 tsp salt
1 dried red pepper, crushed
1 cup long grain white rice, cooked
    and drained
1 1/2 pounds raw shrimp, shelled
    and deveined
6 green onions, chopped

In a large pot, combine water, black-eyed peas, onion, bacon, salt, and red pepper. Cook on low heat for 2 hours. Add in rice. Cook another 20 minutes, stirring occasionally. Stir in shrimp and green onions. Cook an additional 10 minutes.

Serves 4-6

Classic Campfire Spuds

What are those wonderful embers for if not to gently cook plump potatoes to perfection?

1 large Russet baking potato
    per adult
Vegetable oil, olive oil, or one of
    the flavored varieties
salt and pepper
toppings (listed below)

Scrub and rinse potatoes thoroughly. Rub well with oil and add salt and pepper to taste. Place each potato on a sheet of heavy-duty aluminum foil. Bring foil up and over potato and seal tightly. Place in embers around edge of campfire, turning often with long-handled tongs. Cook for 45 to 60 minutes or until tender. You can also grill on your barbecue over medium-hot coals for about the same amount of time.

toppings:
Sour cream and chopped chives
    or parsley
Chopped olives and sour cream
Cream cheese and chopped onion
Crumbled crisp bacon
Sautéed sliced mushrooms
Shredded cheese (cheddar,
    Monterey Jack, mozzarella
    Habanero or another variety)
Chopped green pepper
Lemon-butter sauce
Plain yogurt

SUNDOWN SWEETS

Picnic Apple Dip

1 cup brown sugar; firmly packed
²/₃ cup butter
1 package (8 oz.) cream cheese, softened
1 tsp vanilla
5 pounds apples

In a medium saucepan, blend together brown sugar and butter. Set on the side of your coals until melted, stirring often. Add in cream cheese and stir until melted. Add in vanilla. Cool. Cut apples into quarters, cut out core, and then slice into sections. Dip into caramel-like mixture.

Serves 12

Beach Bunny Cake

This is a very moist cake that needs no frosting, travels well, and makes great finger food. For a fancier dessert cut into larger squares and top with whipped topping or (even better) homemade vanilla ice cream hand cranked by all of those energy-filled kids.

1 cup vegetable oil
2 cups sugar
3 eggs
2 cups grated carrot (about 3 large carrots)
1 small can (8 oz.) crushed pineapple
4 oz. grated coconut
2 cups all-purpose flour
1 tsp salt
1 tsp baking soda
2 tsp vanilla
2 tsp ground cinnamon
²/₃ cup walnuts, pecans, almonds, or hazelnuts, chopped

In a large bowl beat oil and sugar together; add in eggs and continue mixing. Beat in carrots, pineapple, coconut, flour, salt, baking soda, vanilla, cinnamon, and nuts. Pour into a 9 x 13-inch greased baking pan and bake at 350 degrees for 40 to 45 minutes, or until toothpick inserted in center comes out clean.

Serves 12

The Searover's Famous Travelin' Cookies

The Searover is a boat— not a yacht, not a dinghy. On those sunny flat-water fishin' days, the crew takes along these filling treats to nibble on.

1 cup water
2 cups raisins
1 cup shortening
2 cups sugar (I like 1 cup to be
brown sugar)
3 eggs
1 tsp vanilla
4 cups flour
1 tsp baking powder
1 tsp baking soda
1 1/2 tsp salt
1 1/2 tsp ground cinnamon
1/4 tsp nutmeg
1/4 tsp allspice
1 cup walnuts, pecans, almonds or
hazelnuts, chopped

Serves 16

In a small saucepan, add in the water and raisins and boil gently for 5 minutes. Cool. In a large mixing bowl, cream together the shortening, sugar, and eggs. Add raisin mixture and vanilla. In a separate bowl, mix together the flour, baking powder, baking soda, salt, cinnamon, nutmeg, and allspice. Add to raisin mixture and beat well. Add in nuts. Chill dough for an hour or two. Drop a heaping tablespoonful onto greased cookie sheet leaving room between. Bake at 350 degrees for 10 to 12 minutes. These cookies travel very well and taste great even if smashed.

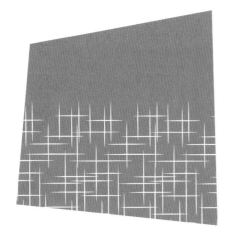

Nancy's Peanut Butter Picnic Cookies

These cookies travel well, especially if you haul them in a plastic container with a snap-on lid. I always make a double batch so there are plenty to nibble on around the bonfire. They're also super topped with a piece of chocolate and a hot toasted marshmallow (like a S'More).

1 cup shortening
1 cup white sugar
1 cup brown sugar
1 tsp vanilla
2 eggs, beaten
1 cup peanut butter
3 cups all-purpose flour
2 tsp baking soda
1/2 tsp salt

In a large bowl, cream together shortening, white and brown sugar, and vanilla. Beat in the eggs and peanut butter. Sift together flour, baking soda, and salt, then add into peanut butter mixture. Flour your hands and form dough into 2 inch balls and place on greased cookie sheet. Smash with a fork twice to make basket weave pattern. Bake at 375 degrees for 10 minutes.

Serves 8

Camper's Cake

This cake travels well, especially since it has no sticky frosting.

1/4 cup + 2 tblsps butter or
    margarine
1 cup + 1 tblsp sugar
2 eggs
1 1/3 cup all-purpose white flour
1 1/2 tsp baking powder
1 tsp baking soda
1 tsp cinnamon
1 cup sour cream
1 package (6 oz.) chocolate chips

In a large bowl, cream together the butter and sugar. Add eggs and mix. In a separate bowl, mix together flour, baking powder, baking soda, and cinnamon. Add to egg mixture and stir well. Add in sour cream and mix until smooth. Pour into a greased and floured (or non-stick) 9 x 13 inch baking pan. Bake at 350 degrees for 35 minutes. Sprinkle chocolate chips over all while cake is still hot.

Serves 12

Walk-the-Plank Cookies

1 cube (1/2 cup) butter or margarine
1 cup graham crackers, crushed
1 cup shredded coconut
1 package (6 oz.) semisweet chocolate chips
1 package (6 oz.) butterscotch chips
1 cup nuts (walnuts, pecans etc.), chopped
1 can (14 oz.) sweetened condensed milk

Serves 12

Melt butter or margarine in a 13 x 9 inch baking pan. Layer remaining ingredients in order listed. Sprinkle condensed milk over all and bake at 325 degrees for 25 to 30 minutes. Cool completely before cutting.

Easy Does It Picnic Cake

1 package (18 oz.) yellow cake mix*
1 package (3 3/4 oz.) vanilla instant
    pudding
4 eggs
3/4 cup vegetable oil
3/4 cup sherry
1 tsp nutmeg or mace
powdered sugar (approximately
    3 tblsps)

*If cake mix includes pudding, eliminate the package of pudding mix.

In a large mixing bowl, combine all ingredients except powdered sugar and beat with electric mixer for 5 minutes at medium speed. Pour batter into a greased 9 x 13 inch baking pan. Bake at 350 degrees for 35 to 45 minutes or until done. Cool 5 minutes before turning onto wire rack. When cooled down, place in plastic container with snap-on lid and sprinkle top with powdered sugar. Goes well with fresh fruit such as strawberries and/or homemade ice cream.

Serves 12

Sunshine Bars

1 cup all-purpose flour
1 cube ($^1/_2$ cup) butter
    or margarine
$^1/_4$ cup powdered sugar
2 eggs, beaten
1 cup sugar
$^1/_2$ tsp baking powder
3 tblsps lemon juice
2 tblsps flour
1 $^1/_2$ cups powdered sugar
1 tsp vanilla
2 tblsps butter or margarine,
    melted
1 tblsp milk

Blend together the first flour, first
butter and first powdered sugar
listed. Press into an ungreased 8 inch
square baking pan and bake at 350
degrees for 20 minutes. In a bowl,
combine eggs, sugar, baking powder,
lemon juice, and the 2 tblsps flour.
Pour into baked pastry shell and
bake for 25 minutes at 350 degrees.
Cool slightly in pan. In a bowl,
combine the 1 $^1/_2$ cups powdered
sugar, vanilla, 2 tblsps melted butter,
and 1 tblsp milk. Spread over baked
cookies in pan and cool before
cutting into bars.

Serves 4–6

Cowabunga Chips

1 box (1 pound) plain graham
    crackers
1 tsp ground cinnamon
1 cup chopped nuts (walnuts,
    pecans, almonds or hazelnuts)
2 cubes (1 cup) butter
2 cups brown sugar
2 tsp vanilla

Lay out graham crackers in a single
layer on an ungreased cookie sheet.
Sprinkle with cinnamon and nuts. In
a small saucepan, over medium
heat, melt the butter and stir in
sugar and vanilla. Boil for 5 minutes,
stirring often. Pour mixture over
crackers. Bake at 350 degrees for 15
minutes. Break into pieces. Carries
well in plastic zip-top bags or
containers. A super treat around
the beachside bonfire.

Serves 12

Cookout Quick-eez

2 cans (7.5 oz.) refrigerator biscuits
$^2/_3$ cup of your favorite jam or
    preserves
1 cup vegetable oil
$^1/_2$ cup powdered sugar

Pat out each biscuit in your hand to
flatten. Place 1 tblsp jam on one half
of the biscuit, fold over and pinch to
seal. Heat oil in a cast-iron skillet or
Dutch oven or grill and fry until
golden brown, turning once. Drain on
paper towels and roll in powdered
sugar. Add $^1/_4$ tsp of ground cinnamon
in the powdered sugar if you desire.

Serves 8

NIBBLES

Travelin' to the Beach Grub

Make this recipe at home and transport in plastic zip-top bags.

1 cup peanut butter
$^1/_2$ cup butter
1 package (12 oz.) semisweet chocolate chips
12 cups Crispex, Rice Chex, Corn Chex or similar cereal
1 package (1 pound) powdered sugar

In a medium bowl, melt together peanut butter, butter, and chocolate chips in microwave, about 4 to 6 minutes. Pour cereal into a large bowl and then pour peanut butter mixture over. Stir to coat cereal well. Pour powdered sugar into a large brown paper grocery bag. Add in chocolate covered cereal and shake well to coat.

Serves 12

Salty Dogs

$^2/_3$ cup butter
$^2/_3$ cup vegetable shortening
2 cups all-purpose flour
2 egg yolks
1 tsp salt
2 tblsp water
2 eggs
4 tsp milk
coarse salt (kosher is best)
caraway seeds

In a medium bowl, cut the butter and shortening into the flour. Add the egg yolks and 1 tsp salt. With a fork, mix in 2 tblsps water. Chill this dough. Roll out dough and cut into pencil-thick sticks about 3 inches long. Beat the eggs with milk and brush the sticks. Place on a cookie sheet and sprinkle with kosher salt and caraway seeds. Bake at 425 degrees until brown (about 10 to 12 minutes).

Serves 4-6

Limey Sailor Snacks

$^3/_4$ cup sharp cheddar cheese, grated
$^1/_4$ cup butter
1 tsp dry mustard
2 tsp Worcestershire sauce
6 slices bacon, cooked until crisp
12 slices thin white bread

Trim crust from bread. In a medium bowl, combine cheese, butter, mustard, and Worcestershire sauce. Drain bacon well, crumble and blend into cheese mixture. Spread mixture on the bread and roll up each slice like a jellyroll, securing with a toothpick. Place on cookie sheet and toast in 325 degree oven, or make a shallow pan out of heavy-duty foil and grill over coals, turning often to toast evenly.

Serves 4-6

Doheny Beach Dip

1 can (16 oz.) refried beans
1 package (8 oz.) cream cheese, softened
2 tblsps green onion, finely chopped
1/2 tsp Tabasco sauce
1/4 tsp garlic salt
1 cup cheddar cheese, grated

In a medium bowl, combine refried beans, cream cheese, onion, Tabasco, and garlic salt. Spread out in a 10 x 12 inch baking dish and sprinkle with the cheese. Cook in the microwave at medium low heat for 10 to 15 minutes or until heated and cheese is bubbly. Serve with tortilla chips, corn chips, potato chips, or bite-size pieces of raw veggies.

Serves 4–6

Cape Shoalwater Dip

1 1/2 cups cooked crabmeat
1 container (16 oz.) sour cream
3 tblsps mayonnaise
1/4 cup blue cheese, crumbled, or a 1 ounce package of blue cheese salad dressing mix
1/2 tsp seasoned salt (such as Johnny's or Lawry's) if you use the fresh blue cheese

In a medium bowl, combine all ingredients well. Chill for at least 2 hours or preferably overnight. Serve with a selection of your favorite crackers.

Serves 4–6

Sea Otter Crest Snacks

1 small can (8 oz.) tomato sauce
1 cup virgin olive oil (vegetable oil is okay)
1 small can (4 oz.) chopped olives
1 cup cheddar or Monterey Jack cheese, grated
1/4 cup sweet onion, finely chopped
1 small can (5 oz.) mushroom pieces, drained well
1/2 tsp salt (or to taste)
1/4 tsp pepper
1/4 tsp garlic powder or 1/2 tsp garlic, finely chopped
1 large loaf French or sourdough bread, sliced

Serves 4-6

In a medium bowl, combine tomato sauce, oil, olives, cheese, onion, mushrooms, salt, pepper, and garlic. Mix well. Consistency will be thick. Spread on bread slices, place on ungreased cookie sheet and bake for about 10 minutes at 350 degrees, more if you like it toasted. Keep in foil pouch and reheat on the edge of your barbecue, hibachi, or on the rocks around your campfire.

Yippee Dogs

1 pound good quality hot dogs
1 1/2 cups catsup
3/4 cup bourbon
1 tblsp sweet onion, grated
1/2 cup brown sugar

Cut the hot dogs into 1-inch sections on the diagonal (looks nicer). In a small saucepan, mix together the catsup, bourbon, onion, and brown sugar. Add in the cut dogs and simmer on low for one hour. Add more bourbon if the sauce becomes too thick. Serve with toothpicks.

Serves 4-6

THIRST QUENCHERS

Blushing Sunset

2 cups powdered orange drink mix
5 cups prepared instant tea
1 cup sugar
1 ½ tsp cinnamon
2 packages (3 oz.) lemonade mix
¾ tsp powdered cloves

Mix together and serve over ice.

Serves 4–6

Totally Perfect Iced Tea

At least 6 hours ahead, preferably overnight, fill a large pitcher with 8 cups cold water. Add 8 to 10 tea bags and let sit in refrigerator at least 6 hours.

Serves 4–6

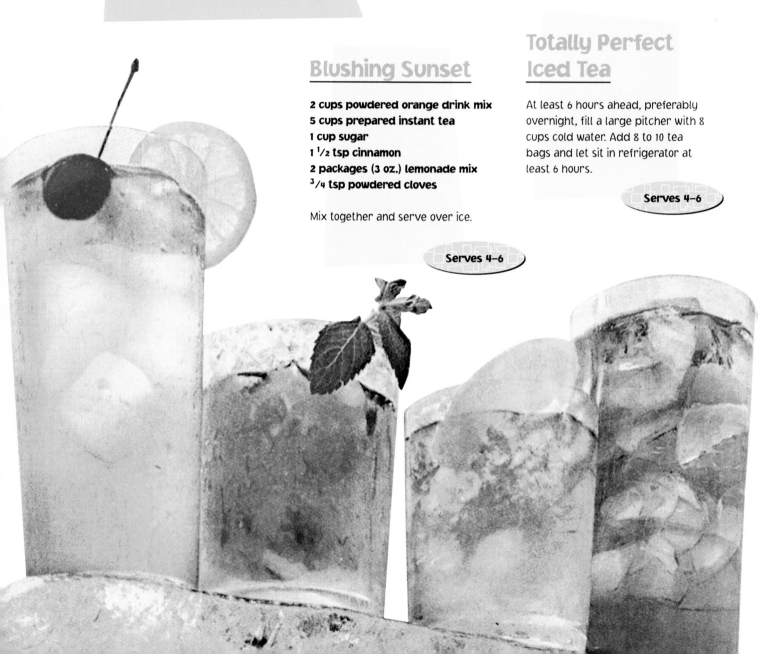

Picnic Classic Lemonade

Basic syrup:
1 ½ cups sugar
1 tblsp lemon peel, finely grated
1 ½ cups hot water
ice
cold water

In a 1-quart jar or similar container with a tight-fitting lid, shake together the sugar, lemon peel and hot water until sugar dissolves. This syrup will keep in your refrigerator for up to 2 weeks.

To make lemonade:
Fill glass (12-oz. size) with ice cubes. Pour in ¼ cup syrup and stir in 3/4 cup cold water.

alternatives:
*Use club soda in place of the cold water.
*Use crushed ice in place of cubes.
*Replace lemon peel and juice with lime.
*For 8 servings, use half of the syrup with 6 cups of water.

Serves 4-6

Sparkling Sea

1 envelope (3.6 oz.) lemon-flavored
iced tea mix
4 cups water
¼ cup fresh mint leaves, crushed
crushed ice or ice cubes
12 bottles ginger ale (12 oz. each),
chilled

In a large pitcher, stir iced tea mix with water until dissolved. Place 1 tsp mint leaves in glass. Add in ice. Slowly pour in ginger ale, stirring gently.

Serves 8-12

Sunrise Ruby Cooler

2 1/4 cups (1 18-oz. can) tomato juice, chilled
1 cup unsweetened pineapple juice, chilled
1 tblsp fresh lemon juice

Mix together well the tomato, pineapple and lemon juice and serve cold.

Serves 4–6

Seadog

1 bottle (7 1/2 oz.) clam juice, chilled
1 can (12 oz.) vegetable juice cocktail
1 tblsp lemon juice
dash of Tabasco (to taste)
ice
lemon wedges

In a medium pitcher, stir together the clam juice, vegetable juice, lemon juice, and Tabasco. Stir well. Serve over ice with a lemon wedge.

Serves 4–6

GOURMET GALLEY

Yucatan Chicken

3 to 3 ½ pound broiler/fryer
    chicken, cut up
1/3 cup butter or margarine
2 cloves garlic, crushed
1 tsp chili powder
¼ tsp ground cumin
½ tsp grated lime peel
2 tblsps lime juice

Rinse chicken and pat dry. Melt butter in a small pan, remove from heat and stir in garlic, chili powder, cumin, lime peel, and juice. Place chicken in a shallow pan or baking dish and baste generously with the marinade. Cook chicken on a lightly greased grill above medium hot coals. Cook chicken skin side up, except for breast pieces. Cook for 15 minutes, basting and turning often. Breast pieces will take about 15 minutes longer. Juices should run clear with no pink near the bone.

Serves 4-6

Shipwreck Skewers

3 tblsps olive oil
2 cloves garlic, crushed
$\frac{1}{4}$ tsp pepper
2 pounds firm-textured fish like
    swordfish, halibut, turbot or
    cod, cut into 1 x 1 $\frac{1}{2}$ inch chunks
salt to taste

In a large bowl, combine oil, garlic, and pepper. Add in fish chunks and turn to coat. Thread fish on metal skewers. Cook on a well-greased grill over medium hot coals. Turn skewers gently several times for about 10 to 12 minutes or until thickest piece of fish flakes when prodded with a fork. Season with salt and serve with relish (recipe follows).

Serves 4–6

Red Relish:

1 small fresh or canned hot green
    chile, stemmed, seeded, finely
    chopped
1 small fresh or canned hot red
    chile, stemmed, seeded, finely
    chopped
1 small fresh or canned yellow chile,
    stemmed, seeded, finely chopped
2 large ripe tomatoes, peeled and
    diced (makes about 1 $\frac{1}{2}$ cups)
1 medium-sized onion, finely
    chopped
$\frac{1}{4}$ tsp salt
1 tsp sugar
1 tblsp red wine vinegar

In a medium bowl, combine chiles, tomatoes, and onion. Add in salt, sugar, and vinegar. Mix well. Cover and refrigerate for 30 minutes or more.

Oysterville Wraps

3 or 4 fresh oysters per person
1 slice (thinly-sliced) lean bacon per
    oyster
salt and pepper
wooden toothpicks
fresh sliced lemons
drawn butter
A-1 sauce
Tabasco sauce

Wrap each oyster in a slice of bacon and secure with a toothpick. Arrange the wrapped oysters in a hinged wire rack and grill quickly over hot coals or campfire until bacon is cooked to your liking. Serve with sliced lemons, butter, A-1 sauce, and Tabasco for dipping.

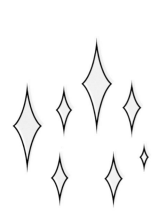

Fish and Seafood

Sleeping Bag Salmon

(per person)
1 salmon filet (approximately ¹/₂ pound)
1 very thin slice of sweet onion (Walla Walla, Maui or Vidalia)
1 very thin slice lemon
¹/₄ tsp garlic
¹/₄ tsp pepper
¹/₂ tsp fresh parsley (or ¹/₂ tsp dried)
¹/₂ tsp olive oil

Place the filet in middle of a sheet of foil. Top with onion, lemon, garlic, pepper, and parsley. Sprinkle with oil. Fold foil in on ends and over top to seal. Grill over medium coals for approximately 15 minutes.

Cove Inn's Clam Soufflé

12 saltine crackers, crushed
1 cup milk
1 cup clams (fresh or canned), chopped
¹/₄ cup butter, melted
1 tblsp Worcestershire sauce
2 eggs, well beaten

Serves 4–6

In a medium bowl, add in crackers and pour milk over. Let stand 20 minutes. Add in clams, butter, and Worcestershire sauce. Mix in eggs last. Pour into 1-quart casserole and bake at 350 degrees for 45 minutes or until firm. This recipe works well if doubled.

Fritter Recipe #1

2 cups clams (fresh or canned),
    finely chopped
1 cup cracker crumbs
$\frac{1}{4}$ tsp cayenne pepper
2 egg yolks, well beaten
$\frac{1}{2}$ tsp salt (to your taste)
$\frac{1}{4}$ tsp coarsely ground black
    pepper (to your taste)
1 tblsp fresh parsley, finely chopped
$\frac{1}{2}$ cup (approximate) clam juice
3 egg whites, stiffly beaten
2 - 3 cups vegetable oil

In a medium bowl, mix together clams, cracker crumbs, cayenne, egg yolks, salt, pepper, and parsley. Add enough clam juice to make a heavy batter (like thick cake batter). Fold in egg whites. Heat oil in your Dutch oven or cast iron skillet. Drop by heaping tablespoon in hot oil. Cook until brown on both sides, turning once. Drain on paper towels. These are so delectable with a green salad, hush puppies (see recipe for "Hush Them Dawgs" on page ___ Chapter 7) or sourdough grilled over those hot coals.

Serves 4–6

Fritter Recipe #2

2 cups clams (fresh or canned), finely
    chopped
2 eggs
1 tsp onion, finely chopped
2 cups raw potatoes, grated
$\frac{1}{2}$ cup biscuit mix (such as Bisquick)
1 tsp salt (to your taste)
$\frac{1}{4}$ tsp pepper (to your taste)
1 cube ($\frac{1}{2}$ cup) butter or margarine

In a medium bowl, mix together clams, eggs, onion, potatoes, biscuit mix, salt, and pepper. In a heavy skillet, melt the butter. Pat together fritter mix in your hands to form small pancakes. Cook in butter, turning once, until browned on both sides. Drain on paper towels and serve hot.

Serves 4–6

PORTSIDE (SALADS 'N' SIDES)

Kahuku Rice Salad

2 cups long grain rice, cooked
4 tblsps vinegar
6 to 8 tblsps olive oil
1 small sweet onion, finely chopped
2 medium tomatoes, chopped
1/4 up green pepper (a mixture of
    green, yellow and red makes for
    more color), finely chopped
3 tblsps fresh parsley, chopped

Cool rice well. In a medium bowl,
combine rice, vinegar, olive oil, onion,
tomatoes, green pepper, and parsley.
Mix thoroughly and chill.

Serves 4-6

China Sea Salad

3 to 4 boneless, skinless chicken breasts
1/4 cup chicken broth
1 head lettuce, shredded
2 tblsps sesame seeds
2 tblsps slivered almonds
3 green onions, finely chopped
1 large can (8.5 oz.) Chinese noodles

dressing:
2 tblsps sugar
1/2 tsp salt
1/4 tsp pepper
1/4 cup peanut or sesame oil
1/4 cup rice vinegar

Simmer chicken in broth until done all the
way through (about 12 minutes). Drain off
broth and cut chicken into bite-sized pieces.
Cool. In a large (gallon size) zip-top plastic
bag, shake together the lettuce, sesame
seeds, almonds and green onions. In a small
bowl, mix together sugar, salt, pepper, oil,
and vinegar until sugar is dissolved. Keep
salad greens and dressing chilled in your
cooler. At your picnic site, add noodles,
chicken, and dressing to greens and toss.

Serves 4-6

Lido Isle Salad

My family spent almost every summertime Saturday at the beaches in southern California. One of our favorite spots to walk around was the tiny elite island of Lido to look at the charming houses crowded together with minuscule yards and expensive yachts dockside.

1 large head broccoli, trimmed and cut into bite-sized pieces
1/2 pound lean bacon, cooked until crisp and chopped
1/2 cup roasted sunflower seeds
1/2 cup raisins
1/2 cup sweet onion, thinly sliced

dressing:
1 cup mayonnaise
2 tblsps white vinegar
1/4 cup sugar

Toss together broccoli, bacon, sunflower seeds, raisins, and onion. In a separate small bowl, mix together mayonnaise, vinegar, and sugar. Whip with wire whisk until mixture is smooth. Pour dressing over salad and toss well.

Serves 4–6

Saltillo (sahl-tee-oh) Salad

1 pound lean ground beef
1 tsp chili powder
1/2 tsp garlic powder
1 tsp salt
1 large head lettuce, shredded
1 cup mixed greens (butterhead lettuce, baby romaine etc.) (optional)
1 tsp dried cilantro or 2 tsp fresh, finely chopped
1 15-oz. can ranch-style beans
1/2 red onion, thinly sliced (about 1/2 cup)
2 large ripe tomatoes, chopped
1 pound (2 cups) cheddar cheese, grated
1 1/4 cups Catalina-style dressing
1 large ripe avocado, peeled and sliced
2 cups corn chips

Serves 4–6

Brown ground beef in a skillet. Pour off fat and drain on paper towels. Sprinkle with chili powder, garlic powder, and salt. Cool. Toss together lettuce, greens, cilantro, beans, onion, tomatoes, and cheese. Chill for at least 30 minutes. Drizzle with dressing. Garnish with avocado slices and corn chips.

Castaway Cucumber Soup

Although you must make at home, this delicious soup travels well and makes a classy first course. Imagine an elegant picnic on the dunes with a romantic sunset as the backdrop.

1 tblsp olive oil
1 medium onion, thinly sliced
2 large cucumbers, unpeeled, diced
2 cups chicken bouillon
1 tsp cornstarch
3 tblsps water
1/2 tsp salt
1/4 tsp pepper
1 cup heavy cream
1/2 cup dry Vermouth

In a medium skillet, heat the olive oil and sauté the onion until soft. Turn down heat and add in cucumbers and bouillon. Mix together cornstarch and water in a small dish or jar until dissolved. Blend into soup and add in salt and pepper. Simmer gently for 20 minutes, mixture should be slightly thick. Cool. Whirl in blender in small batches until smooth. Stir in cream and Vermouth. Chill thoroughly and transport in thermos bottle.

Serves 4-6

Stormfront Soup

8 oz. tomato sauce
2 cups beef bouillon
5 1/2 cups water
4 cups tomato juice
dash of Tabasco sauce
1 1/2 tsp salt
1/4 tsp dried basil
1/4 tsp dried oregano
1/2 tsp dried parsley
4 tsp sugar
1/2 cup sherry
2 tblsps fresh chives (optional), finely chopped
1/4 cup sour cream

In a large pot, combine tomato sauce, bouillon, water, juice, Tabasco, salt, basil, oregano, parsley, sugar, and sherry. Heat to just below boiling. Garnish with chives and/or sour cream if you like. Travels well to beachside parties.

Serves 4-6

93

Sopa Tierra (Soup of the Earth)

2 large ripe tomatoes or 1 cup canned
tomatoes
1 large clove garlic, chopped
1 medium onion
3 tblsps butter or margarine
4 cups cooked kidney or pinto beans
or 2 cans (15 oz.), undrained
2 cups chicken broth
2 chicken bouillon cubes
1/2 tsp chili powder
1 tsp salt (adjust to taste)
1/4 cup Muenster cheese, cubed
3 strips thick lean bacon, cooked until
crisp and crumbled

In your blender or food processor, on medium speed, whirl together the tomatoes, garlic, and onion until the consistency of salsa. Heat butter in a large heavy skillet and pour in tomato mixture. Cook on high heat for 5 minutes. Whirl the beans and their juices in the blender on medium speed until smooth. Add to tomato mixture and heat 5 minutes more, stirring occasionally. Add the chicken broth, bouillon cubes, chili powder, and salt. Cook for another 10 to 15 minutes on low heat. Put a few cubes of cheese in the bottom of each soup bowl or mug. Pour soup over cheese and garnish with bacon. Serve with tortilla or corn chips.

Serves 4–6

Too-Easy-To-Be-True Campside Soup

1 can (10 3/4 oz.) condensed tomato
soup
1 can (10 3/4 oz.) condensed green
pea soup
12 oz. beer
1/4 teaspoon garlic powder
1/4 teaspoon salt (optional)
1 can (4 1/2 oz.) tiny shrimp
1 1/2 cups half and half or cream

In a sturdy campfire pot, dump in soups, beer, garlic and salt. Stir well over medium coals, stirring until smooth. Simmer for 5 minutes. Just before serving, add undrained shrimp and half and half. Heat thoroughly but do not boil. Serve with crusty sourdough bread toasted on your grill.

Serves 4–6

Crabpot Chowder

2 tblsps butter or margarine
1 small onion, finely chopped
2 cups dry white wine
1 1/2 pounds potatoes, peeled and
cubed
1 tsp salt
1/2 tsp dried thyme
1 cup water
dash of cayenne pepper
2 1/2 cups milk
1 pound crabmeat
Parsley for garnish

In a large pot, melt butter and sauté onion until tender. Add in wine, potatoes, salt, thyme, and water. Bring to a boil. Reduce heat to low and cook until potatoes are done (about 20 minutes). Add cayenne pepper, milk and crabmeat. Heat thoroughly, but do not boil. Ladle into mugs and garnish with parsley.

Serves 4–6

Barnacle Bart's Bread

1 cup butter, softened
4 oz. blue cheese, crumbled
2 tsp onion, finely chopped
1 tsp dried rosemary leaves,
crushed
1 tsp dried basil leaves, crushed
2 tblsps fresh parsley, finely
chopped, or 1 tblsp dried
1 large loaf (1 pound) French bread

In a small bowl, combine butter, cheese, onion, rosemary, basil, and parsley. Slice bread diagonally about $3/4$ inch apart without cutting all the way through the bottom crust. Spread herb/butter/cheese mixture between slices and wrap loaf in a sheet of heavy-duty aluminum foil. Grill over low heat about 15 minutes or until heated thoroughly, turning occasionally.

Serves 4–6

Seacliff Café's Veggie Casserole

3 medium carrots, peeled and sliced
(sliced on the diagonal looks nice)
$1/2$ pound green beans, sliced
1 medium yellow summer squash,
sliced
1 medium zucchini, sliced
$1/2$ head cauliflower, broken into
flowerets
$1/4$ cup butter
1 large clove garlic, finely chopped
1 cup chicken broth
1 tsp salt
$1/4$ tsp pepper

On a large sheet of heavy-duty aluminum foil, arrange all of the vegetables. In a saucepan, melt 3 tblsps of the butter and sauté the garlic until tender but not browned. Stir in broth, salt, and pepper. Pour mixture over vegetables and dot with remaining butter. Seal up foil tightly and grill over medium-hot coals for about 30 minutes. Shake packet gently every 10 minutes.

Serves 4–6

Sailboat Sweets

1 ½ cups (³/₄ pound) butter or
    margarine
4 pounds sweet potatoes or yams,
    peeled and shredded
¹/₄ cup sugar
¹/₄ cup tequila
2 tblsps lime juice
¹/₂ tsp salt
dash of black pepper

In a baking pan (about 12 x 16 inches),
melt butter. Mix potatoes in with
butter and sprinkle with sugar.
Continue cooking uncovered until
potatoes begin to caramelize (takes
about 15 minutes). Turn occasionally
with a spatula. Stir in tequila and lime
juice. Continue cooking for another 3
to 5 minutes. Season with salt and
pepper. This is a great dish to make
ahead and reheat over the coals
while cooking your steaks.

Serves 8

Walla Walla Onion Casserole

¹/₂ cup butter or margarine
4 medium Walla Walla sweet onions,
    sliced about ¹/₄-inch thick)
15 saltine crackers, crushed
1 can (10 ³/₄ oz.) cream of
    mushroom soup
2 eggs, beaten
1 cup sharp cheddar cheese,
    shredded
¹/₂ to ³/₄ cup milk

Serves 4–6

Melt butter in a skillet. Sauté onions
over medium heat until tender and
transparent. Keep aside 4 tablespoons
cracker crumbs. Lightly grease a 2-
quart casserole dish and layer bottom
with remaining cracker crumbs. Drain
butter off of onions and layer them
over crumbs. Cover with soup. Sprinkle
cheese evenly over soup. Combine eggs
with reserved crumbs and spread over
cheese layers. Pour milk over all. Bake
at 350 degrees for 30 minutes.

SUNSETTERS (DESSERTS)

Tipsy Fruit

This recipe is about as simple as you can get and yet there's a bit of elegance. The amount of liqueur depends upon the amount of fruit and your personal taste. I recommend approximately 4 tablespoons of liqueur per 12-ounce can of fruit. The fruit tastes best when very cold (chill well in your ice chest beforehand).

blueberries with Kirsch
frozen raspberries (thawed) with Cointreau
canned pear halves (drained) with Marsala
canned apricots (drained) with Rum
canned peach halves with Bourbon

Serves 4–6

Grilled Fruit

You can simply baste the fruit with melted butter or make a sauce of $^1/_2$ cup ($^1/_4$ pound) melted butter mixed with 1 tsp ground cinnamon or a combination of cinnamon and ginger.

apples: Core and peel (if desired), cut into halves. Grill about 10 to 12 minutes.

apricots: Cut fresh apricots into halves and discard pits. Thread on skewer making sure fruit lies flat. Grill about 4 to 6 minutes.

pineapple: Cut a fresh pineapple lengthwise into 8 sections. Place in a shallow pan and drizzle with about 1 tblsp honey per section. Let stand for about 30 minutes before grilling.

bananas: Leave unpeeled. Slit skin about 3 inches long, squeeze open enough to drizzle in 1 tblsp honey mixed with $^1/_4$ tsp ground cinnamon. Let stand for about 30 minutes before placing on grill and cooking for about 8 minutes.

papayas: Peel then cut crosswise into 3/4-inch-thick rings or cut lengthwise into quarters. Remove and discard seeds. Grill 5 to 8 minutes.

peaches: Drain canned peach halves. Drizzle each half with about 1 tblsp honey, or 1 tblsp honey combined with $^1/_4$ tsp ground cinnamon, or brush with melted butter and sprinkle with about 1 tsp brown sugar. Grill about 4 minutes if using canned, 6 to 8 minutes if fresh.

pears: Peel, if desired. Cut small ones into halves lengthwise, large ones into 3/4-inch wedges. Core. Thread on skewers, making sure fruit lies flat. Grill about 6 minutes for wedges, 10 to 12 for halves.

Classy Jack's Fruit Fondue

This is a fun and somewhat fancy dessert to finish off your beachside barbecue. When the coals burn down to embers, set pots of these sauces on the grill and dip away.

For each person, allow $^3/_4$ cup fresh fruit, such as grapes, apple chunks, peach slices, pear, papaya, or strawberries; and 4 to 6 1-$^1/_2$ inch cubes of pound cake, lady fingers, plain biscotti, or butter cookies.

Citrus Honey Sauce

$^1/_2$ **cup ($^1/_4$ pound) butter, melted**
1 cup whipping cream
$^1/_4$ **cup sugar**
$^1/_4$ **cup honey**
$^1/_4$ **cup orange marmalade**
$^1/_4$ **cup orange liqueur**

Combine the butter with cream, sugar, honey, and marmalade. Bring to a gentle boil over the coals. Move to edge of fire and stir in orange liqueur. Keep warm.

Serves 4-6

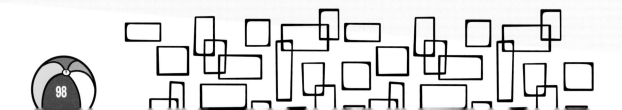

98

Chocolate Lover's Dip

12 oz. milk chocolate, chopped, or
   milk chocolate chips
3/4 cup whipping cream
3 tblsps coffee-flavored liqueur

In a heatproof pot, melt chocolate
over low coals, stirring in cream until
mixture is smooth. Stir in liqueur. Keep
stirring, being careful not to scorch
the chocolate.

Serves 4–6

Ensenada Yacht Racers

1 can (8 oz.) crushed pineapple
2 eggs, beaten
3/4 cup sugar
3/4 cup flour
1 tsp baking powder
1/4 tsp salt
1/2 cup coconut, shredded
1/2 cup walnuts, chopped
1/2 cup dates, pitted and chopped
3-4 tsp powdered sugar

Dump pineapple in a sieve and press
out as much of the juice as possible.
(If you don't, the batter will be too
sloppy.) In a medium bowl, beat
together eggs and sugar. Sift
together flour, baking powder, and
salt. Add flour mixture to eggs and
sugar. Fold in coconut, walnuts, and
dates. Add in pineapple. Mix well.
Pour in greased 9-inch square baking
pan at 350 degrees for 30 minutes.
Cool. Dust with powdered sugar and
cut into squares. This is such a great
recipe, I always bake at least a double
batch.

Serves 4–6

Summertime Cloud

assorted cheeses (cheddar, Jack,
   Gouda, Camembert, etc.)
1/3 cup apricot preserves or orange
   marmalade
1 carton (8 oz.) sour cream
1/4 cup walnuts, finely chopped
3 tblsps milk
assorted slices of fruit (bananas,
   apples, pears)
Fruit Fresh (commercial product
   that prevents fruit from turning
   brown)
toothpicks

Make ahead at home and keep cool in
ice chest.

In a large bowl, cut fruit into slices
and sprinkle with Fruit Fresh. Cut
cheese into chunks and transport in
covered flat container. Place
preserves in small bowl and stir in
sour cream and walnuts. Add enough
milk to make of dipping consistency.
Cover and chill at least 1 hour. Serve
with fruit and cheese to dip.

Serves 4–6

Fine Fare Fruit Soup

This delicious soup can be made ahead at home or in your RV It can be served either hot or cold. Our gang prefers it cold with a dollop of homemade vanilla ice cream.

$^1/_2$ **pound dried apricots**
$^1/_2$ **pound dried prunes**
$^1/_2$ **pound raisins**
1 cinnamon stick, or $^1/_2$ tsp ground cinnamon
2 $^3/_4$ quarts water
$^1/_2$ **to 1 cup sugar (adjust to your own taste)**
2 tblsps cornstarch or quick tapioca
$^1/_4$ **cup cold water**

Serves 4-6

In a large pot, simmer together the apricots, prunes, raisins, cinnamon, water, and sugar until fruit is tender, about 30 minutes. If using cornstarch, dissolve in the $^1/_4$ cup water and slowly pour into fruit mixture and continue simmering until slightly thick (about 10 minutes). Can be served with a dollop of ice cream or whipped cream or over rice pudding, angel food cake or pound cake.

Beach Basket Bread

5 cups all-purpose flour
8 tsp baking powder
1 tsp baking soda
1 tsp salt
2 eggs
2 cups buttermilk
1 cup sugar
1 cup walnuts, pecans, almonds, or hazelnuts, chopped
1 pound dried apricots, chopped
4 tblsps butter, melted

Serves 4-6

In a large bowl, combine flour, baking powder, baking soda, and salt. In a separate bowl, beat together eggs, buttermilk, and sugar. Add to flour mixture. Fold in nuts and apricots. Butter 2 loaf pans (2 $^3/_4$ x 3 $^3/_4$ x 12 $^1/_2$ inches) or 6 small (2 x 3 $^1/_2$ x 6 inches). Bake at 350 degrees for 1 hour for large loaves, 45 minutes for small. Test for doneness with toothpick. This rich dessert bread needs no icing or garnish.

FLOTSAM 'N' JETSAM (APPETIZERS)

Skipper Jack's Stuffed Eggs

12 hard-boiled eggs, peeled
12 fresh mushrooms. finely chopped
2 tblsps green onion, finely chopped
2 tsp fresh parsley, chopped
2 tblsps butter
2 tblsps sherry

Serves 4–6

Cut eggs in half and remove yolks. In a small bowl, toss together the mushrooms, onion, and parsley. In a saucepan, heat the butter and add in the mushroom mixture and sherry. Sauté 5 or 6 minutes over medium heat. Mash the egg yolks and add into mushroom mixture. Fill empty egg white halves and chill well.

Sea Devil Eggs

Remember! Eggs in any form must be kept cold in your ice chest or RV fridge.

12 hard-boiled eggs, peeled
1/2 cup crabmeat, cooked, flaked
2 tsp Parmesan cheese, grated
3 tblsps butter
2-3 tblsps mayonnaise
2 tblsp chives, finely chopped
1 tblsp parsley, finely chopped
dash of Tabasco (optional)
1/2 tsp salt (adjust to your taste)
1/4 tsp coarsely ground black pepper
(adjust to your taste)
paprika

Serves 4–6

Cut the eggs in half and remove yolks. In a small bowl, combine egg yolks with crabmeat, cheese, butter, mayonnaise, chives, parsley, Tabasco, salt, and pepper. Mix well. Spoon into egg white halves and dust with paprika.

Whidbey Island Smokey Dip

1 ½ pounds smoked salmon, skinned, boned and flaked
1 cup mayonnaise (don't use a cheap brand)
½ cup sour cream
2 tblsps fresh parsley, finely chopped
½ tblsp prepared mustard
2 tsp celery, finely chopped
2 tsp sweet onion, finely chopped
1 clove garlic, finely chopped
dash of Worcestershire sauce
assorted crackers, chips and/or raw vegetables

In a medium bowl, combine fish, mayonnaise, sour cream, parsley, mustard, celery, onion, garlic, and Worcestershire sauce. Blend well. Chill at least 1 hour, overnight if possible. Serve with crackers, chips, and/or raw vegetables.

Serves 4–6

Oysterville Cracker Snacks

Oysterville, Washington, is a charming tiny village of historic houses and a thriving oyster business. The beautiful Willapa (will-ah-pah) Bay is the rich "farm" where millions of oysters are raised and harvested.

1 oz. package ranch dressing mix
³/₄ tsp dry dill weed
¼ cup salad oil
12 oz. package plain oyster crackers

In a medium bowl, mix together the dressing mix, dill, and oil. Add in crackers and toss gently. Bake in a 250 degree oven for 20 minutes. Stir carefully for 10 minutes.

Serves 4–6

103

Sunburned Bread

1 pound (about 2 cups) fresh ripe
   tomatoes, peeled, cored and
   finely chopped
¹/₂ cup red onion, finely chopped
1 tblsp dry or 2 tblsps fresh basil
   leaves, finely chopped
¹/₄ cup olive oil
6 slices crusty Italian or French
   bread, about ¹/₂ inch thick
¹/₂ tsp salt
¹/₄ tsp pepper

Drain tomatoes well. Place tomatoes in
medium bowl and mix well with the
onion, basil, and 2 tblsps oil. Use
remaining 2 tblsps oil to brush each
slice of bread on both sides; toast
bread on grill or in flat basket rack
over campfire. Heap tomato mixture
on toast, salt, and pepper and serve
at once.

Serves 4-6

Dover Coasters

1 small can (6 oz.) crabmeat,
drained
³/₄ cup mayonnaise
1 cup cheddar cheese, grated
¹/₄ cup green onions, finely
chopped
1 tsp Worcestershire sauce
6 to 8 English muffins

Serves 4-6

In a medium bowl, mix together well
the crab, mayonnaise, cheese, onion,
and Worcestershire sauce. Spread
mixture on top of muffin halves and
broil about 3 minutes, or until light
brown and bubbly. For campside,
heat muffins by sitting on edge of
grill. You can also substitute 1 small
can (4 oz.) chopped black olives in
place of the crab.

PORTABLE POTABLES

Both of these drinks travel well because you can haul the frozen base in your cooler and by the time you get to your beachside picnic it has thawed to about the right slushiness.

Seaside Slush

(For a crowd)
5 cans (12 oz. each) frozen lemonade
5 cans (12 oz. each) frozen orange juice
3 $3/4$ cups water
1 can (16 oz.) apricot nectar
1 package (10 oz.) frozen strawberries
2 bottles (2 liters each) lemon-lime carbonated soda

In a large container, mix the lemonade, orange juice, water, nectar, and strawberries. Pour into clean empty milk cartons and freeze for at least several hours, preferably overnight. To serve, place frozen mixture in a large bowl (I use a big stainless steel bowl, but a cheap popcorn bowl sold at dollar stores works well). Break up mixture with a spoon and cover with the soda.

Serves 16

Castaway Tropical Punch

6 cups water
4 cups sugar
3 cups orange juice (not from concentrate)
$1/2$ cup fresh lemon juice (okay, bottled will work)
2 cans (46 oz. each) pineapple juice
6 ripe bananas, mashed
3 bottles (2 liters each) ginger ale

In a large pot at home, boil together water and sugar until syrupy (about 30 minutes). Take off heat and cool. Mix in orange juice, lemon juice, pineapple juice, and bananas. Freeze in clean empty milk cartons. When ready to serve, thaw until slushy, add ginger ale and serve immediately.

Serves 16

Crabfest Cooler

2 cans (6 oz. each) frozen lemonade
2 cans (6 oz. each) frozen orange juice
1 pint cranberry juice
1/2 pint Hawaiian punch base
1 can (6 oz.) frozen grape juice
8 1/2 cups water
3 quarts ginger ale or lemon-lime soda

In a large bowl, mix together the lemonade, orange juice, cranberry juice, Hawaiian punch, grape juice, and water. When ready to serve, add well-chilled ginger ale or soda.

Serves About 20

Fish House Punch

$3/4$ cup sugar
2 quarts light rum
4 oz. peach brandy
1 quart fresh lemon juice
1 quart brandy
1 quart club soda
5 pound ice block

At home, combine sugar, rum, peach brandy, lemon juice, and brandy at least 2 hours before beach party. Stir occasionally. Just before serving, add club soda and pour over ice.

Serves 12-18

Perfect Peachy Slurp

Make this at home or in your RV kitchen.

2 cups water
1 1/2 cups sugar
1 can (6 oz.) frozen lemonade
2 packages (16 oz. each) frozen peaches
1 1/4 cups vodka (optional)
1/3 cup lime juice
lemon-lime soda

In a medium saucepan, combine water and sugar and bring to a gentle boil. Cook until sugar dissolves, stirring a few times. Cool. Add in lemonade concentrate and stir. Whirl peaches in blender until smooth. Mix peaches with lemonade mixture and add vodka and lime juice. Freeze in shallow pan or large zip-top plastic bag. Keep on ice. When ready to serve scoop in enough slush to fill glass half full then fill up with soda.

Serves 4-6

Special Around-the-Campfire Coffee

4 cups brewed coffee
¹/₄ tsp anise seed

Top with whipped cream, vanilla ice cream, frozen whipped topping or a chunk of semisweet chocolate.

Serves 4–6

Company Coffee

For iced coffee, brew regular coffee but double the amount of coffee grounds. Serve over ice cubes and offer cream and sugar.

Alternate method: Brew coffee as usual, but serve over ice cubes made from coffee. Serve with cream and sugar.

Serves 4–6

Chrome Coffee

2 cups cold strong coffee
1 pint lemon sherbet
2 tblsps grenadine syrup

Whip together with a blender or by hand coffee, sherbet, and grenadine right before serving.

Serves 4–6

107

Balboa Island Offshore Breeze

(per person)
1 $\frac{1}{4}$ oz. vodka
4 oz. cranberry juice
4 oz. grapefruit juice

Pour vodka, cranberry juice, and grapefruit juice over crushed ice.

White Sandy Beach

(per person)
1 $\frac{1}{2}$ cups cold strong coffee
3 tblsps sugar
1 banana, cut in pieces
$\frac{1}{2}$ pint vanilla ice cream

Whip together coffee, sugar, banana, and ice cream right before serving. Dig out the blender in your RV for this if you can.

Barbecue with a View

GRILLIN' IT · BURGERS 'N' DOGS
OTHER GRILLED GOODIES

GRILLIN' IT

Beachcomber Baby Back

1 ½ tblsps butter or margarine
1 medium onion, chopped
½ cup water
½ cup chili sauce
½ cup dark molasses
½ cup brown sugar, firmly packed
¼ cup apple cider vinegar
2 tblsps Worcestershire sauce
2 tsp Wright's concentrated Hickory Seasoning (Liquid Smoke)
2 tsp dry mustard
½ tsp pepper

½ tsp paprika
3 to 4 pounds pork baby back ribs, trimmed of fat

In a medium skillet, melt butter and add in onion. Cook on medium heat until tender. Stir in water, chili sauce, molasses, sugar, vinegar, lemon juice, Worcestershire sauce, Liquid Smoke seasoning, mustard, pepper, and paprika. Bring to a boil over high heat. Reduce heat and simmer uncovered for about 30 minutes. Remove from heat. Barbecue meat over medium-hot coals, starting with meat side up. Brush often with sauce. If you have a cover on your grill, put it down and adjust dampers for low, even heat. Cooks ribs, basting often, until meat near bone is no longer pink (about 1 to 1 ¼ hours).

Serves 4–6

Sea Rover Steaks

½ tsp dried instant onion, or 1 tsp fresh
3 tblsps wine vinegar
½ cup vegetable oil
1 tsp seasoned salt (such as Johnny's or Lawry's)
6 cube steaks (approximately ¼ pound each)
6 slices sharp cheese
3 tsp butter or margarine
6 hamburger buns

In a shallow dish, soak onion in vinegar for about 15 minutes. Add in oil and seasoned salt. Mix well. Place steaks in mixture and turn over a few times to coat. Cover and let sit in cool place for an hour or so. Grill over very hot coals about 2 minutes per side. For the last minute, place a slice of cheese over steak to melt. While grilling steaks, butter buns and toast on cooler edge of coals. Serve steaks on hot buns. Goes well with a green salad and watermelon wedges.

Serves 6

Clear the Decks

The delectable smell of this chicken will certainly clear the decks, whether it's the deck of your yacht or the deck of your beach cabin.

1 10 $^3/_4$ - oz. can onion soup, undiluted
$^1/_2$ cup catsup
$^1/_4$ cup vegetable oil
$^1/_4$ cup apple cider vinegar
2 -3 tblsps light brown sugar
1 tblsp Worcestershire sauce
dash of Tabasco sauce
2 cloves garlic, finely chopped
2 broiler/fryer chickens (2 $^1/_2$ to 3
    pounds each), cut-up

In a medium saucepan, combine soup, catsup, oil, vinegar, brown sugar, Worcestershire, Tabasco and garlic. Simmer over medium heat, stirring often, until heated through. Cool. Place chicken in a large 1 gallon zip-top plastic bag. Pour half of sauce over chicken and chill for at least 4 hours, preferably overnight. Drain sauce off of chicken and grill over hot coals for 15 minutes, turning to brown both sides and basting often with the reserved sauce. Continue grilling for approximately 30 minutes or until chicken juices run clear.

Serves 4-6

Churasco Chicken

1 12 - oz. can beer
1 tsp salt
$^1/_4$ tsp pepper
3 tblsps lemon juice
dash of Tabasco sauce
$^1/_2$ tsp orange flavoring extract
1 tsp orange peel, grated
2 tblsps brown sugar
1 tblsp dark molasses
2 broiler/fryer chickens (2 $^1/_2$ to 3 pounds each), halved

Serves 8

In a small bowl, combine beer, salt, pepper, lemon juice, Tabasco, flavoring, peel, sugar, and molasses. Mix well. Place chicken in a large 1 gallon zip-top plastic bag and pour in half of the marinade. Refrigerate several hours or overnight. Drain marinade from chicken and grill over hot coals for about 45 minutes, basting often with reserved sauce. Turn often. Cook until juices run clear.

Coastland Kebabs

$^1/_4$ cup olive oil
$^1/_3$ cup lemon juice
2 tsp salt
1 tsp pepper
2 cloves garlic, finely chopped
1 tsp dried rosemary leaves, crushed
2 - 2 $^1/_2$ pounds beef shoulder or top round
    roast, cut into 1-inch cubes
1 large sweet onion, cut into chunks
2 large green peppers, cut into chunks
16 whole cherry tomatoes
32 large pitted black olives

Serves 8

In a small bowl, combine olive oil, lemon juice, salt, pepper, garlic, and rosemary. Mix well. In a large 1 gallon zip-top plastic bag, place marinade, meat, onion, and green pepper. Seal and toss lightly. Refrigerate at least 4 hours, turning occasionally. Drain off marinade and thread meat, onion, green peppers, tomatoes, and olives on 16 skewers. Grill over hot coals, turning often until meat is no longer pink.

BURGERS 'N' DOGS

A LITTLE BURGER KNOW-HOW

1 Don't buy the leanest ground beef as it quickly becomes too dry and tasteless when grilled.

2 A burger cooked rare or medium rare is simply not safe. Cook hamburger for 18 to 20 minutes (9 to 10 minutes per side), until the juices run clear.

3 Resist the impulse to smash the patties down with your spatula as this releases all of those yummy juices.

Acapulco Burgers

1 ½ pounds ground beef
1 egg, well beaten
2 tblsps sweet onion, finely chopped or 1 tblsp instant minced onion
¼ cup chili sauce
1 garlic clove, finely chopped, or ½ tsp. garlic powder
1 tsp salt
¼ tsp pepper
good quality hamburger buns or sourdough rolls
4 slices cheese (jalapeno Jack, cheddar, habanero or your favorite)
4 thick tomato slices
shredded lettuce
salsa

Serves 4–6

In a medium bowl, mix together the ground beef, egg, onion, chili sauce, garlic, salt, and pepper. Form into four patties and grill over high heat for 18 to 20 minutes or until juices run clear. Serve on buns or rolls with cheese, tomato slices, lettuce, and salsa in place of mayonnaise and catsup.

Beachcomber Burgers

1 1/2 pounds ground beef
1 egg, well beaten
1 small can (4 1/2 oz.) mushroom pieces, drained,
   or 1/2 cup fresh mushrooms, sliced, sautéed
1/4 cup red wine
thickly sliced French bread
1/4 cup blue cheese, crumbled

In a medium bowl, mix together the ground beef, egg, mushrooms, and wine. Form into 4 patties. Grill as directed above. Put each burger on a slice of French bread, sprinkle with blue cheese and top with second slice of bread. These burgers have so much flavor, you probably won't want to offer the usual toppings such as tomatoes or lettuce.

Serves 4–6

Big Al's Pizza Burgers

1 1/2 pounds ground beef
1 egg, well beaten
4 tblsps Mozzarella cheese, shredded (Provolone
   or Ricotta will work)
4 tblsps Italian salami or pepperoni, finely chopped
1 tblsp oregano
1 tsp garlic powder
1 tsp salt
1/4 tsp pepper
Italian rolls
4 thick slices of tomato

Serves 4–6

In a medium bowl, mix together the ground beef, egg, cheese, salami or pepperoni, oregano, garlic, salt, and pepper. Form into 4 patties and grill according to above directions. Serve on nice crusty Italian rolls or similar sturdy bread. Top with tomato.

B.C. Burgers

1 1/2 pounds ground beef
1 tsp salt
1/4 tsp pepper
hamburger buns
4 tblsps blue cheese
4 slices Canadian bacon
steak sauce

In a medium bowl, mix together the
ground beef, salt and pepper. Form
into 6 patties and grill as directed.
Put on a bun. Top each patty with
cheese and a slice of Canadian bacon.
Grill over hot coals in a cast iron
skillet. Offer steak sauce and top with
remaining half of bun.

Serves 6

Nana Kuli's Kona Burger

2 pounds ground beef
1 tsp onion powder (or 2 tblsps sweet Maui onion,
  finely chopped)
1 tsp lemon juice
1/4 cup soy sauce
1/2 tsp pepper
2 tblsps dry sherry
1 clove garlic, grated or 1/2 tsp. garlic powder
1/4 tsp powdered ginger

Serves 6-8

In a medium bowl, mix together well the ground beef and onion.
Form into 6 to 8 patties. In a small bowl, combine lemon juice, soy
sauce, pepper, sherry, garlic, and ginger. Grill as per directions on
page... Baste often with sauce. Experiment with different types of
buns like sourdough, sweet, thickly sliced French bread, or rye.
Serve with Kahuku Rice Salad (recipe on page 94, chapter 7)

Burgers for a Bonfire Bash

This recipe makes 30 hamburger patties.

10 pounds ground beef
$^1/_4$ cup olive oil
1 medium sweet onion, finely chopped
1 cup catsup
1 cup chili sauce
2 tblsps dry mustard
3 tblsps Worcestershire sauce
$^2/_3$ cup wine vinegar
$^1/_4$ cup brown sugar
1 cup water
1 tsp garlic powder
2 tsp salt
1 tsp pepper

Serves 20-30

Form ground beef into patties. In a large saucepan, heat oil and sauté onion until tender. Add in catsup, chili sauce, mustard, Worcestershire sauce, vinegar, sugar, water, garlic, salt, and pepper. Mix well and simmer for 15 minutes. Cook burgers according to directions and baste generously on both sides with the sauce.

Gold Beach

1 $^1/_2$ pounds ground beef
$^1/_4$ cup soft bread crumbs
$^1/_3$ cup Teriyaki sauce
1 egg
4 tblsps sweet onion, finely chopped, or 2 tblsps instant minced onion
$^1/_4$ tsp pepper
$^1/_2$ cup sharp cheddar cheese (Tillamook is my personal choice), shredded

In a medium bowl, combine the ground beef, breadcrumbs, sauce, egg, onion, and pepper. Shape into 12 patties. Sprinkle cheese over 6 patties, leaving a $^1/_2$-inch margin around the edges. Top with remaining patties and pinch together edges to seal in the cheese. Grill according to the directions on page 114, being extra careful when you flip the burgers. This recipe goes well with classic baked beans, potato salad, foil-baked fries or even a nice green salad.

Serves 6

Hilo Dogs

1 cup apricot preserves (for a change, try
   using orange marmalade)
$^1/_2$ cup tomato sauce
$^1/_4$ cup cooking sherry
1/3 cup apple cider vinegar
2 tblsps soy sauce
2 tblsps honey
1 tblsp salad oil
1 tsp salt
1 tsp freshly grated ginger root or $^1/_4$ tsp
   ground ginger
1 can (12 oz.) pineapple slices, drained
2 pounds hot dogs

Serves 6–8

In a medium saucepan, combine the preserves, tomato
sauce, sherry, vinegar, soy sauce, honey, oil, salt, and
ginger. Simmer gently for 5 minutes. Grill the hot dogs
slowly, turning and basting with the sauce until heated
through and glazed (about 8 minutes). The last few
minutes, start grilling the pineapple rings, basting with
the sauce. Heat remaining sauce and serve the hot dogs
with the grilled pineapple. Offer buns if you like and a
tossed salad.

Hang Ten Dogs

2 tblsps vegetable oil
1 (^{1}/$_2$ cup) small sweet onion, chopped
1 pound hot dogs or frankfurters
1 can condensed tomato soup
^{1}/$_3$ cup water
1 ^{1}/$_2$ tblsps bottled steak sauce
1 tsp. prepared mustard
dash of Tabasco
Coney Island or hoagie buns, buttered and toasted

In a medium skillet, heat oil and sauté onion until tender but not browned. Cut the franks into thirds. Add franks, soup, water, steak sauce, mustard, and Tabasco into skillet with sautéed onions. Simmer gently, uncovered, about 15 minutes or until sauce has thickened. Stir occasionally. Scoop franks and sauce onto buns and serve.

Serves 4–6

Dune Dogs

^{1}/$_4$ cup vegetable oil
2 cups sweet onions, finely chopped
1 ^{1}/$_4$ cups (1 - 14 oz. bottle) catsup
^{1}/$_2$ cup water
^{1}/$_4$ cup brown sugar
1 tblsp apple cider vinegar
2 tblsps Worcestershire sauce
^{1}/$_2$ tsp dry mustard
1 tsp salt
1 tsp Wright's Concentrated Hickory
   Seasoning (Liquid Smoke)
2 pounds hot dogs
hot dog, hoagie, or other buns

In a large saucepan, heat oil and sauté onion until tender. Add in catsup, water, brown sugar, vinegar, Worcestershire sauce, mustard, salt, and Liquid Smoke. Simmer, uncovered, 15 minutes. In the meantime, grill franks over hot coals, turning often until lightly browned. Place franks in buns and spoon on sauce.

Serves 6-8

OTHER GRILLED GOODIES

Surfer Dude Ribs

1 tsp salt
$^1/_4$ tsp coarsely ground black pepper
1 lemon, thinly sliced
$^1/_2$ cup onion, finely chopped
1 tsp chili powder
1 tsp celery salt
$^1/_2$ tsp ground ginger or 1 tsp freshly grated
$^1/_4$ cup Worcestershire sauce
$^1/_4$ cup wine vinegar
1 cup catsup
2 cups hot water
$^1/_4$ cup brown sugar
$^1/_4$ to $^1/_2$ tsp Tabasco sauce (according to your taste)
5 pounds lean pork spareribs

In a medium saucepan, combine salt, pepper, lemon, onion, chili powder, celery salt, ginger, Worcestershire sauce, vinegar, catsup, water, brown sugar, and Tabasco. Simmer on low heat for an hour or so. Place ribs on grill, rounded side up. Add a small handful of dampened mesquite chips to the coals and close hood of barbecue or cover with a sheet of heavy foil. Turn ribs every few minutes for approximately 2 hours. Baste with above sauce for an additional 30 minutes.

Serves 4–6

Campfire Ribs

3 pounds pork spareribs
¼ cup Wright's Concentrated
    Hickory Seasoning (Liquid Smoke)
1 small onion, chopped
1 large clove garlic, finely chopped
1 tsp. dried parsley or 2 tsp fresh
    parsley
1 ½ tsp salt
¼ tsp dried rosemary
¼ tsp dried ginger
¼ tsp pepper
½ cup dry sherry
2 tblsps brown sugar
2 tblsps tomato paste

Serves 4–6

Cut ribs into servings (1 or 2 per person). Brush well with Liquid Smoke and place in a shallow baking dish. Combine onion, garlic, and parsley and sprinkle over the meat. Combine salt, rosemary, ginger, and pepper and sprinkle over the meat. Cover with foil or plastic wrap and let stand overnight. In a small bowl, combine sherry, sugar, and tomato paste. Grill ribs over a slow fire as above, basting often with the sauce.

Steak Teriyaki

This is an easy recipe that can be prepared ahead at home, wrapped in aluminum foil and hauled in an ice chest. The meats can be marinated in a tightly sealed and chilled container while you are traveling.

1 large clove garlic, minced
½ onion, finely chopped
¼ cup soy sauce
1 tblsp powdered ginger (optional)
¼ cup dry white wine
2 pounds boneless steak, cut in thin
    strips across grain*

*Meat will slice easier if partially frozen.

Serves 6-8

Combine garlic, onion, soy sauce, ginger, and wine in a shallow glass dish. Marinate meat in the mixture at least two hours, preferably overnight. Thread on skewers and wrap tightly in foil. Grill over hot coals 3 to 5 minutes.

Cape Blanco Broil

4 lean pork sausages
4 chicken livers
2 slices lean bacon
4 small lamb chops
1 pound London broil steak (or club steak)
4 medium tomatoes
1 tsp garlic salt
1/2 tsp pepper
1/2 tsp tarragon or 1/2 tsp dill

Over your medium charcoal fire, cook the sausages first for about 20 minutes. Sprinkle all of the following meats and the tomatoes with the garlic salt and pepper and either tarragon or dill. Cut bacon into 4 pieces. Wrap each chicken liver in bacon, secure with a toothpick, and grill for 15 minutes. Grill the lamb for 10 minutes. Grill the London broil steak for 10 minutes and slice into 4 portions. Grill tomatoes for 5 minutes. Divide all into 4 equal portions and serve with Foiled Garlic Bread (recipe follows).

Serves 4

Foiled Garlic Bread

1 large loaf French bread
1 stick real butter, room temperature
1 tsp pureed garlic or 1 tsp garlic powder
1/2 tsp salt
1 tsp dried parsley
dash of oregano

Slice bread lengthwise. In a small bowl, mix together the butter, garlic, salt, parsley, and oregano. Spread both sides of the bread and wrap in aluminum foil (heavy type is best). Heat on side of your barbecue grill, being careful to heat evenly. Takes about 10 minutes. Unwrap and slice through diagonally.

Serves 4-6

Fire 'N' Fare

THE FINE ART OF TOASTING MARSHMALLOWS

After a delicious seaside meal, when the sun dips down over the waves in vivid colors, it's time to break out the marshmallows.

Hopefully by now you have a nice bonfire that has burned down to a glowing heap of coals. You already checked out the rules for building that fine fire. Many beaches allow them only on the beach itself, or only in designated fire pits, because of the danger of grass fires among the dunes. There are store-bought metal toastin' sticks, also used for hot dogs, or the old standby of straightened-out wire hangers.

Store-bought are best, as they usually have the safer wooden handles.

Impale one to three fat marshmallows on the end of the stick. Be careful not to handle them too much or they'll flop around and end up as "sundowners," toasted only on one side. Keep them out of the smoke and flames or your reward will be a "flamin' Cajun biscuit," black as a lump of charcoal. Hold the white puffs about 12 to 18 inches from the glowing coals, turning slowly and constantly until light golden brown. Gentle is the keyword or

just as your delicious treat is ready to eat, the whole works will plop into the flames with a fiery poof and a resounding groan from all. If you're one of those non-gourmet rowdies who like their marshmallows cremated, you are on your own. Use caution pushing the toasted gems onto a plate, or better yet, into your eager mouth, because that melted spun sugar is plenty hot enough to burn. As always, use extra care and supervision with the kiddies when around any fire or hot foods.

Indian Beach Sundaes

1 package (10 oz.) marshmallows
1 jar (16 oz.) or 1 bottle (24 oz.)
  chocolate syrup
1/2 gallon vanilla ice cream

Toast marshmallows over hot coals.
Pour 1/4 cup hot fudge or chocolate
syrup into a small bowl (a mug works
well for kids). With a fork, scoot hot
toasty marshmallows off skewer onto
chocolate and swirl with spoon to
marble together. Spoon in a big scoop
or two of ice cream and yummm.

Sea Dog Delight

Okay, okay, so these are sort of an
offshoot of S'Mores, but these are an
easier version for the little kids.

1 package (10 oz.) marshmallows
1 package (10.5 to 14.4 oz.) chocolate
  drop cookies (such as Fudge
  Shop Grasshoppers or Mother's
  Fudge) and/or chocolate-covered
  graham crackers

Alternate marshmallows with cookies
on skewer. Toast over coals until
marshmallows and cookies turn soft.
Fork off skewers onto paper plates.
An alternative is to use firm fruit
chunks in place of the cookies
(apples, pears, pineapple, and
papaya work well).

Tropical Kabob

1 store bought pound cake or angel
  food cake
1/2 cup sweetened condensed milk
  or 1/2 cup honey and 1 tblsp
  lemon juice
1 package (14 oz.) flaked coconut

Cut pound or angel food cake into 1
1/2-inch cubes. Dip in condensed milk
or a mixture of honey and lemon
juice. Roll cubes in coconut. String on
skewers and toast over very hot
coals, turning often. This may be too
tricky for little kids.

Index